9|4

Co-operation in action

Collaborative initiatives in the
world of information

Co-operation in action
Collaborative initiatives in the world of information

Edited by
Stella Pilling

and

Stephanie Kenna

facet publishing

Published by
Facet Publishing
7 Ridgmount Street
London WC1E 7AE

Facet Publishing (formerly Library Association Publishing) is wholly owned by CILIP: the Chartered Institute of Library and Information Professionals.

First published 2002

British Library Cataloguing in Publication Data

A catalogue record for this book is available from the British Library.

ISBN 1-85604-424-6

Typeset in 9.5/13pt New Baskerville and Franklin Gothic Condensed by Facet Publishing.
Printed and made in Great Britain by MPG Books Ltd, Bodmin, Cornwall.

Contents

Foreword

I warmly welcome this timely review of the current state of co-operation between libraries, information providers and other cultural institutions. I am encouraged by the progress so far, which I regard as an important step towards developing a skilled, educated, well-informed and employable workforce.

The overall aim of the Department for Culture, Media and Sport (DCMS) is to improve the quality of life for all through cultural and sporting activities and to strengthen the creative industries. Clearly, libraries, museums and archives play a major role in tackling the wider objectives of social inclusion, regeneration and lifelong learning, underpinning education in the broadest sense.

Though diverse, libraries, museums and archives share at least one common attribute: they are organizations rich in content, with the power and resources to stimulate, motivate and inspire all those wishing to extend their knowledge. Their importance in the life of the nation is shown by the fact that more than 60% of adults belong to a public library and that more people visit museums than theme parks or pop concerts.

A key message of the Library and Information Commission's report *Empowering the learning community*, published in March 2000, was the need to develop partnerships amongst all the various bodies involved. It argued strongly that closer collaboration between libraries and educational institutions would mean greater and more effective support for learners and potential learners.

As the contributions to this book reveal, a great deal of headway has been made in breaking down barriers, opening up dialogue and improving services, but there is still a long way to go. Co-operation is not easy – it takes hard work and persistence. Funding for such co-operative work, attempting as it does to operate across sectors, can be problematic. In an increasingly complex world, however, it is crucial that we develop fresh approaches in order to engage people in learning and to encourage the creative use of collections and resources, wherever they may be.

Tessa Blackstone
Minister of State for the Arts

Introduction

Compiling a book about co-operation, particularly co-operation involving libraries, museums and archives, is not an easy task. Like motherhood and apple pie, co-operation is universally regarded in the library and information field as a Good Thing. Information professionals are all aware that, in order to serve the needs of their users, readers and customers, it is essential to work with others. This is all the more necessary in the light of the continuing increase in the number of items published every year both in traditional hard copy and electronically. No library is an island — nor ever has been — and it is no longer realistic, cost-effective or indeed logical for any major library or information provider to work alone.

This collection emphasizes the crucial role played by libraries, museums and archives, both separately and together, in support of lifelong learning and in underpinning the move towards increased social inclusion and economic regeneration.

Because of its all pervading influence, however, co-operation is difficult to define precisely – it can mean different things to different people at different times. It can sometimes appear as if co-operation is more talked about than acted upon, exactly because a co-operative mentality is so much part of the professional furniture. This is not true, as the contributions to this book prove. Active co-operation is alive and kicking.

We are delighted to have been able to bring together a range of distinguished contributors, known for their involvement in, and support for, co-operation in the library and information sphere. From their different backgrounds and perspectives, they provide a snapshot of recent and current co-operative activity, both across the different library sectors, and with the museums and archives domains. The inclusion of information about museums and archives, and their developing relationships with libraries, is one of the unique features of this book.

Building on the United Kingdom's co-operative landscape, as surveyed by Education for Change and Acumen for the British Library's Co-operation and Partnership Programme, the book focuses primarily on activity within the UK, but also looks in general terms at international issues, drawing comparisons with, and lessons from, initiatives in other countries. Within the field of preservation in particular, fundamental issues are not constrained by domain-specific concerns, nor by national boundaries, and international, as well as cross-domain, co-operation has long been a key feature.

The picture of co-operation is not, of course, uniform. In some sectors there is a long history of co-operation and an understanding of earlier co-operative activity is necessary to explain current developments. Elsewhere, new policies and new technology are driving new collaborations and partnerships. Chapters 3 and 7, on Resource and on E-co-operation respectively, focus on the cutting edge of co-operative activity and are thus more visionary in nature, while current developments in higher education and the UK regions are more fully explained in their historical context.

The meaning and definition of co-operation can differ, but it is clear that, in practice, there is a great deal in common, and readers will notice some recurring themes in the contributions to this book. Major issues are approached from different perspectives, for example, co-operation in the higher education sector features in the chapters dealing with funding and preservation as well as in the chapter specifically focusing on developments in academia. The book can be read as a whole, providing a detailed and comprehensive insight to the overall scene; equally, each chapter stands alone and can be read separately.

Following the scene-setting chapter detailing the perspective on co-operation from the British Library, Chapter 2 by Moore and Carpenter reviews the current co-operative landscape within the United Kingdom. The third chapter, by Griffiths and Mackay, describes the increasingly important role of Resource: the Council for Museums, Archives and Libraries in the cross-domain co-operative agenda. Within the context of the growing emphasis on regional issues, Brewer, in Chapter 4, surveys some of the regional developments in co-operation within the last few years. Naylor in the following chapter discusses co-operation in the academic sector with particular reference to organizations such as CURL and SCONUL. The chapter on preservation by Kenna and Shenton, brings together, for the first time, a comprehensive snapshot of major initiatives, nationally and internationally, across sectors, domains and disciplines. Law's chapter on e-co-operation highlights the role that technology can play in helping libraries, museums and archives avoid many of the issues that have bedevilled traditional resource sharing. Funding for co-operation is, and always has been, problematic. Milne in Chapter 8 draws attention to the need to ensure that co-operative work, crossing as it often does traditional boundaries, is imaginatively and adequately funded. The final chapter by Cornish examines the concept of international co-operation and whether and to what extent it is possible or realistic.

At the end of the chapters specific references for follow-up reading and research are provided. In addition we have provided a separate cumulative list of websites. The URLs were checked and were correct at 31 October 2001. A list of acronyms is also included.

Co-operation is about breaking down the artificial boundaries between institutions, between sectors and between domains in order that better services can be provided. Our involvement in the British Library's Co-operation and Partnership Programme over the last three years has convinced us of the absolute necessity for partnership and sharing and has shown us that working collaboratively — although not without its problems — can be fun!

Stella Pilling
Stephanie Kenna

Acknowledgements

The editors would like to thank a number of people in connection with this book. We are indebted to the authors, who responded so enthusiastically to our invitation to contribute and who adhered valiantly to the somewhat tight timetable, and to Henry Girling, who meticulously checked the website URLs and produced the final version of the typescript for us. We would also like to thank Helen Carley and colleagues at Facet Publishing for their support and patience.

List of contributors

Stuart Brewer

Stuart Brewer is a freelance consultant with nearly 40 years' experience in the library and information domain. Following public library posts in London, the East Midlands and Cumbria, he was City Librarian and Arts Officer, Newcastle upon Tyne, from 1980 before moving to the Library and Information Commission as Executive Secretary, 1995–6. From 1996 he has worked with Pat Wressell Associates, Capital Planning Information Ltd (CPI) and Instant Library Limited, where he is also Director of the CPI Library and Information Policy Seminars Programme. He was closely involved in the transformation of the Northern Regional Library System into Information North (1989), and with CPI and Instant Library Limited he has worked on regional strategies for libraries and on cross-domain assignments involving libraries, museums and archives.

Julie Carpenter

Julie Carpenter, Director of EfC, has been an independent consultant for 11 years. She set up a consulting and research company after 12 years of working in the British Council's London headquarters as an adviser and Information Projects Officer, and as Assistant Director (Books and Libraries), Greece. In the early 1990s, the focus of her work was on information sector review, policy development and institutional strengthening and she carried out research for the British Library Research and Development Department as well as working for the Department for International Development and other international development agencies. In the mid-1990s she became the project manager for the project MOBILE (1994–7) and, with the focus now firmly on Europe, she participated in several research projects in library and information services, health and education in the UK. Recently she has been working in the UK on the impact of electronic information services and the digitization of collections, as well as with cultural heritage sector organizations such as the National Maritime Museum, providing consulting and market research services.

Graham P. Cornish

Graham Cornish joined the (now) British Library (BL) in 1969. He held a number of posts in different parts of the Library, and since 1983 he was responsible for copyright issues within the BL. Since 1986 he managed much of the Library's involvement with IFLA, for whom he acted as Director of the Universal Availability of Publications Programme. Graham is a Fellow of CILIP: the Chartered Institute of Library and Information Professionals. Since 1999 he has been Regional Vice-President (Europe) of the Commonwealth Library Association and he was president of the (UK) Library Association (now CILIP) for the year 2000.

Vivien Griffiths

Vivien Griffiths retired in 2001 as Acting Director of Leisure and Culture at Birmingham City Council. She had a long career in public libraries, specializing in services to children, young people, education and lifelong learning. She has been President of the Society of Chief Librarians and a Board member of Resource: the Council for Museums, Archives and Libraries.

Stephanie Kenna

Stephanie Kenna graduated from Oxford in geography and undertook research at Manchester University into the historical geography of South Lancashire before becoming a graduate trainee at Durham University Library. Since joining the British Library in 1975 she has worked in several areas including reader services, preservation and the former Research and Innovation Centre, where she was Research Analyst for the preservation research programme and the heritage sector. Stephanie has been a member of the Library's Co-operation and Partnership Programme since its establishment in 1999. She has oversight for preservation issues and funding opportunities and is responsible for liaising with the archive and museum communities. She also administers the Library's fund that supports co-operative projects.

Derek Law

Derek Law is head of the Information Resources Directorate at the University of Strathclyde and a Professor in its Centre for Digital Library Research. As the only librarian ever to be a member of the Computer Board he has been actively involved in the development of digital libraries at national and local level for over a decade and has served on numerous national and international committees in this area. A regular author and lecturer both nationally and internationally, he is also Treasurer of the International Federation of Library Associations (IFLA) and is a Fellow of the Royal Society of Edinburgh.

Neville Mackay

Neville Mackay was Chief Executive of Resource: the Council for Museums, Archives and Libraries from 1999 to 2002. Before joining Resource, Neville spent many years as a senior policy adviser in Whitehall. His last post was as Head of Libraries, Information and Archives Division within the Department for Culture, Media and Sport. Before that he had spells in a number of government departments including the Department for the Environment and the Department for Education.

Ronald Milne

Ronald Milne has been Director of the Research Support Libraries Programme since October 1998. Responsible for an initiative that promotes collaborative, cross-sectoral, work, he has had an appreciation of what can be achieved by library co-operation since the earliest stages of his career. He was previously Assistant Director of Library Services at King's College London and has also held posts at Trinity College Library, Cambridge, Glasgow University Library and on the University of London Library Resources Co-ordinating Committee. He trained at Cambridge University Library. Ronald was a member of the British Library/Higher Education Task Force and has been active nationally and regionally in the University, College and Research Group of CILIP. He contributes to professional journals and is a Fellow of CILIP: the Chartered Institute of Library and Information Professionals.

Nick Moore

Nick Moore is the Managing Partner in Acumen, a company he established in 1983 to explore a wide range of issues concerned with the use of information in society. During the 1980s his work focused on two main issues: the changing nature and structure of the information workforce and the development of techniques for measuring the performance of libraries and information services. More recently his work has been concerned with the analysis of policies supporting the development of information societies and the application of information and communication technology to improve the performance of government. He was appointed the first Professor of Information Management at Birmingham Polytechnic in 1987. In 1989 he joined the Policy Studies Institute to establish a programme of information policy research. In 1995–6 he was associated with the British Council, studying the development of information societies in East Asia and advising the Council on its information strategy in that region. In 1998 he rejoined Acumen to continue his research and consultancy. He was appointed as Professor of Information Policy at City University in 1998 and Visiting Professor in Information Strategy at the University of Brighton in 2000. He is a Visiting Fellow of Bristol University. Nick Moore is also Chairman of the Help for Health Trust, which is a major provider of consumer health information.

Bernard Naylor

Bernard Naylor was educated at Balliol College, Oxford (Modern Languages) and University College London (Librarianship). Having previously worked at the Bodleian Library (1964–6), the University of London Institute of Latin American Studies (1966–74) and as Secretary of the Library Resources Co-ordinating Committee of the University of London (1974–7), he was University Librarian of the University of Southampton from 1977 until his retirement at the end of 2000. In addition to being President of The Library Association (now CILIP) for 2001, he is a non-Executive member of the Board of the British Library (since 1995), a Trustee of the National Manuscripts Conservation Trust (since 1995) and a member of the NESLI Steering Group (as well as Chair of the NESLI Advisory Board), the RSLP Steering Group, and the Steering Group of the UK National Union Catalogue Study.

Stella Pilling

Stella Pilling has worked for the British Library since 1979. After graduating in German and French she began her professional career as a graduate trainee with Birmingham Public Libraries, before moving on to Renfrew District Libraries in Scotland, where she was Depute Chief Librarian. Based at the British Library's Boston Spa site, she has been responsible for a range of functions including acquisitions, customer services, publishing, marketing and business development. She is now a member of the Library's Co-operation and Partnership Programme, set up in 1999 to administer a co-operation fund and to act as a focal point for co-operative and partnership activity.

Helen Shenton

Helen Shenton is Deputy Director of Scholarship and Collections at the British Library (BL). She is responsible for the preservation and conservation of the BL's collections, both traditional and digital. She is project chair of the Digital Library System, which is an innovative project to store all the BL's digital material, and sits on a number of advisory boards, including the National Preservation Office, SCOLD-Pres and the Digital Preservation Coalition. Helen joined the BL in 1998 after 14 years at the Victoria and Albert Museum, where she was most recently Assistant Head of Conservation. She has taught and examined conservation courses, edited journals, lectured and published on a wide range of preservation and conservation subjects. She is an accredited member of the UKIC, IPC and a Fellow of the International Institute of Conservation.

1

The view from the British Library: the national library perspective

Stella Pilling and Stephanie Kenna

Co-operation: new trend or old *modus operandi*?

Co-operation is not a new concept in the world of libraries, museums and archives. Although co-operation may be deemed by many to represent the triumph of hope over experience, those involved in the provision of information services of all kinds know that it is essential to work with others in order to be able to satisfy the needs of users, readers, researchers, enquirers, customers and visitors. Working together is perceived to be an integral part of the ethos of the information world and the effectiveness of British libraries and information services is in no small part due to a long tradition of formal and informal co-operation. As the universe of information and documents continues to expand at an unimaginably speedy rate, and as organizations struggle to keep up with developments in their field of interest, libraries have to work together in order to cope.

Co-operation is certainly not new for the British Library (BL), which, as the national library of the UK and one of the world's leading research libraries, has a long tradition of collaborative working, a tradition that has been strengthened in recent years with the establishment of its Co-operation and Partnership Programme (BLCPP). The BLCPP was set up in 1999 as a direct result of recommendations stemming from the Library's 1998 Strategic Review (British Library, 1999), with the remit to align the BL's approach to co-operation more closely with the strategies being developed by related organizations, both nationally and internationally. Specifically, co-operation in the areas of collection development, collection management and access was seen as the main priority.

In 2001 the BL's second consultation exercise, *New strategic directions* (British Library, 2001), reinforced the Library's vision of the future. Responses from stakeholders soundly endorsed the strategic proposals that it contained, giving the BL the confidence to move ahead with the three enabling strategies put forward:

working in partnership; focusing on users; exploiting the web. The BLCPP has a central role in the first of these, with the task of initiating and maintaining effective partnerships with organizations having a stake in the BL's activities and enabling all involved to achieve far more in partnership than they could ever aspire to on their own. Collaborative working with many cultural, 'memory' institutions, including museums and archives – not just with other libraries – is now clearly on the agenda for the BL.

Central to the BL's new strategy is the desire to make its own collections, as well as those of other institutions, both in the UK and overseas, more accessible to everyone. In order to achieve this vision of global access, the BL is working in partnership with other libraries, becoming more in tune with the changing needs and priorities of users and making the web central to all its activities. A key element of the BL's strategy is the closer integration of its activities with the national and international library network, enabling it to work more effectively with many other collecting institutions in collecting, preserving, recording and providing access to its holdings. The BL believes that it is no longer realistic, or even logical, for any major library in the world to work alone to achieve its goals and ambitions. Co-operation is not an option, but an imperative, informing the BL's strategy and approach in a number of key arenas.

Closer co-operation and partnership, when implemented effectively and not just for their own sake, have the potential to reduce unnecessary duplication of effort, to extend provision into areas not previously covered, and to ensure value-for-money across the publicly-funded sectors. Expenditure can be targeted more cost-effectively in the knowledge of what other organizations are doing and purchasing. In terms of collection development, co-operation should bring with it the confidence that another library, for example, will be acquiring items in a particular field and ensuring permanent access, preservation and storage, thus freeing others to concentrate in different spheres. Effective co-operation can also provide more comprehensive information to users about the availability of relevant resources, resulting in better use of time and avoidance of unnecessary journeys.

The British Library's Co-operation and Partnership Programme

Since its formation, The BLCPP has improved the range and scope of collaborative and partnership activities with a significant number of bodies in the library, museum and archive domains. It has begun to pursue co-ordinated approaches to collecting and making available library and cultural resources, as well as working with other, relevant organizations in specific subject and discipline areas. These studies and activities will provide a sound basis to support the development of collection management strategies at a national level.

The Programme's main strands of activity have, to date, encompassed the following areas:

- identifying and reviewing existing co-operative activities
- establishing a dialogue with the library community
- pursuing co-operative and partnership initiatives with other organizations
- funding cross-sector and cross-domain projects through its co-operation fund.

Within this framework, the BLCPP's key areas of specific activity include:

- seeking the extension of legal deposit legislation to include non-print material
- seeking agreement, with other institutions, on the shared collection of, and access to, foreign publications
- participating in national initiatives on resource discovery
- aiming to improve the collection of, and access to, local publications
- supporting a national strategy on retrospective catalogue conversion
- improving access to collections through collaborative digitization initiatives
- developing shared responsibility for the preservation of the national intellectual and cultural record in both print and non-print formats
- developing shared approaches to the bibliographic control of UK publications
- encouraging and developing cross-sectoral and cross-domain links.

Much of the Programme's detailed work so far has been to investigate, develop and support co-operation between the BL and other institutions bilaterally or multilaterally within individual subjects or focusing on specific formats.

The British Library's co-operation fund

Since the BLCPP was set up in 1999, there have been two Calls for Proposals for projects seeking financial support from this fund. To date, 29 individual projects have been supported. The first Call sought collaborative and partnership approaches to:

- collecting and making accessible library and information resources
- the retention and preservation of resources to ensure long-term access
- activities and mechanisms aimed at ensuring resources can be identified and located.

In general terms, projects were to contribute to and facilitate the development of a more distributed and co-ordinated approach to resource sharing and service provision at the national and regional level. The theme of the second Call was aimed particularly – though not exclusively – at public libraries and, in the event, a high proportion of the successful projects did involve public libraries working with organizations in other sectors to serve the needs of lifelong learners and to facilitate the widening of access to resources for the general public.

Mapping the co-operative landscape

An early decision for the BLCPP was to commission a research report to examine examples of co-operative activities in the library and information domain. Results from the survey are described in Chapter 2 of this book. The research team focused on current and recent initiatives, specifically within the UK, but also drawing on similar projects undertaken in other parts of the world. One element of the study was a literature search, which revealed a clear need for a more strategic approach to co-operation. An important finding from this research was the lack of co-operation across domains: there was little evidence of libraries, museums and archives working together in a practical context. The importance of inter-lending as the main driving force of co-operation among libraries was seen to be declining as a result of the development of national systems and networking. Interoperability between different automated systems emerged as the next logical step for libraries in all sectors in order to maximize the range and effectiveness of co-operative services. In this context, the BLCPP has been making efforts to bring the various stakeholders involved in automated interlending systems together, as part of the Making the Links initiative.

Concord

Concord (**www.bl.uk/concord/**) is the website of the BL's Co-operation and Partnership Programme. It was formally launched in July 2000 with the aim of bridging the gap between libraries, museums and archives by acting as an information exchange, encouraging co-operation and raising awareness of existing collaborative initiatives. An important function of the website is to promote co-operation and to act as a forum for the exchange of experience regarding collaboration, particularly in the cross-domain context. In addition, it provides advice on preparing funding applications to a range of bodies, including the BL's own co-operation fund. On the Concord site can also be found details of successfully funded co-operative projects as well as numerous links to other relevant websites.

Working with others

Cross-domain and cross-sector

The BL has unique and demanding responsibilities, which it is seeking to fulfil amidst a rapidly developing environment. Changes are taking place daily in the world of digital content, political agendas and user expectations. Collaborative working is a *sine qua non* and the BL is building on and expanding its relationships with well established partners as well as seeking out new ones. A seamless interface between the BL's own research collections and those of higher education is a major priority, one that is being actively pursued at a strategic level by the BL in conjunction with the Research Support Libraries Group (RSLG), chaired by Sir Brian Follett (see Chapter 8). There is a growing awareness of a revitalized role for the public library sector in the context of the People's Network and the National Grid for Learning, and real opportunities exist to map the collections of the public library sector on a regional basis.

An important new partner was created in April 2000, when Resource: the Council for Museums, Libraries and Archives was set up by the government. Resource's task is to harness the central role played by museums, libraries and archives in supporting and sustaining cultural and intellectual endeavour, providing the strategic direction necessary to enable the sector's collections and services to enrich the lives of all citizens. Chapter 3 gives an insight into Resource's vision, objectives and achievements to date. Since its formation, the BL has developed a close working relationship with Resource, which amongst other things has co-funded four BLCPP projects in 2001–2, namely those with a cross-domain emphasis. Resource's commitment to improving the experience of those who currently use the nation's libraries, archives and museums is one that the BL supports wholeheartedly. Together with Resource and CILIP: the Chartered Institute of Library and Information Professionals, the BL is jointly funding a post of regional development officer to act as the focus at national level for regional developments across the library and information domain in England. All three organizations are very aware of the importance of close cross-domain links.

Cross-domain collaboration – collaboration and partnerships with museums and archives – represents, in many respects, a new area for the BL, though it has always maintained dialogue with other national institutions and organizations in the museum and archival communities – for it also holds archival collections and displays its treasures in exhibition galleries. The BL's Chief Executive, Lynne Brindley, spoke at the keynote plenary session at the MDA (formerly the Museum Documentation Association) conference in September 2001, and joined a panel of leading figures

5

in politics, museums and the media to answer questions from delegates on the issues surrounding museums and galleries at the Museums Association conference in October 2001. In addition, the BL has been investigating the potential for co-operation and partnership in specific disciplines, such as natural history materials with the Natural History Museum Library and in the history of science and medicine with the Science Museum Library. In the current political climate, which positively encourages cross-domain working, the BL is now beginning to investigate and explore areas in which it might fruitfully work more closely in partnership with the museum and archive communities.

The BLCPP has funded projects that involve archives or museums: for example, contributing to the archival map of the UK through the National Council on Archives-led project *The Missing Link*, which is surveying specialist record repositories; and enabling the Theatre Museum to contribute collection level descriptions of its collections to the *Backstage* project funded by the Research Support Libraries Programme (RSLP). BLCPP is also funding a number of cross-domain projects, involving libraries, museums and archives, such as *Pictures in print*, which brings together maps and views of County Durham from across the domains as well as from the BL's own collections.

The BL currently leads the cross-domain initiative *Full Disclosure*: the national strategy for the retrospective conversion of catalogue and documentation data and the retrospective cataloguing or documentation of non-current acquisitions in libraries, archives and museums throughout the UK. The *Access to Archives* programme led by the Public Record Office, in which the BL is also a partner, forms one strand of the national strategy. Through a wide variety of activities, including the promotion of a framework document endorsed by the Heritage Lottery Fund (HLF), which forms the basis of HLF policy on projects in this area, *Full Disclosure* aims to guide funding bodies and applicants to funders on strategic priorities for retrospective catalogue conversion and retrospective cataloguing. *Full Disclosure* is also supported by HLF involvement in the programme of advisory workshops piloted by the Full Disclosure Implementation Group.

In March 2001 the Full Disclosure Implementation Group, with support from the BLCPP, the Consortium of University Research Libraries (CURL), the Library and Information Co-operation Council (LINC), Resource and RSLP, issued a tender for a study to assess retrospective conversion priorities in libraries, archives and museums in the UK. The Cultural Heritage Consortium was awarded the contract to undertake the study, and commenced with a wide-ranging process of consultation, through face-to-face meetings and interviews and the circulation of a consultation paper among practitioners and professional groups. Their report will be published in 2002.

In the regions

Although the BL has always been involved with organizations in the regions, in particular, with the regional library systems, it has more recently embarked upon a programme of much closer collaboration with regional bodies, particularly with those having a cross-domain role. Meetings have been held with representatives of the North East Museums, Libraries and Archives Council (NEMLAC), which is the regional strategic body and development agency for museums, library and archive organizations in the north east; with Birmingham City Libraries, Museums and Art Galleries and with The Libraries Partnership – West Midlands (TLP–WM), which brings together the libraries and information services of 14 local authorities and eight universities in the West Midlands. A joint bid for an initiative entitled *Reaching the Regions* has been submitted by the BL, the North East and West Midlands Regions to the Treasury's 'Invest to Save' budget.

Two regionally based initiatives have received funding from the BLCPP co-operation fund: the Co-East Plus project and Widening Access to Resources in Merseyside (WARM) in Liverpool. Co-East Plus will bring together the resources of the library and information sectors within the east of England and develop the capacity to enable partners from the museums and archives domains to participate in resource sharing in the longer term. WARM will provide a mechanism for seamless searching across the catalogues of libraries in all sectors of Liverpool; these catalogues contain over three million items and will form a key resource for lifelong learners in the city. Both Co-East Plus and WARM will also offer the opportunity for the BL's products and services to be accessed by a wide range of potential users, alongside content with a strong regional flavour. A description of other regional co-operative activities can be found in Chapter 4.

Discussions have begun with organizations in the regions, in particular with those in the public library sector, to consider how to improve the collecting of, and access to, UK local publications. Research has shown (Harris, Feather and Evans, 2000) that a relatively small percentage of all local publications are deposited with the BL. There is a clear need for an effective model that would facilitate co-operative arrangements at national, regional and local levels to improve the coverage of local publications and to ensure their recording in the *British national bibliography*. The BL is also very much involved with the established NEWSPLAN programme, which is addressing the collection and preservation of local newspapers on a national scale, with particular regard to preserving at-risk historic local newspapers.

With public libraries

Since its creation in the early 1970s, the British Library has been providing services to support public libraries, particularly in the context of underpinning the sector's role with regard to lifelong learning, economic prosperity and quality of life. Currently, over 200,000 requests per annum, 10% of total UK requests to the BL's Document Supply Centre, come from UK public libraries. At a more strategic level, the BL is now working towards building an effective partnership with the public library sector, with which it has a shared agenda in terms of widening access, supporting those involved in learning in any form and contributing to regional strategies and economic development. Within this context, stronger ties are being developed with the Society of Chief Librarians (SCL), which represents all public library authorities in England and Wales. In order to work more effectively across traditional library boundaries, the SCONUL/SCL/British Library Access and Referral Taskforce was set up in April 2001 to explore mechanisms for improving access for library users of all kinds in the UK and to develop a framework of reciprocal agreements within and across national, regional and local authority boundaries.

The major theme of BLCPP's Call for Proposals 2000 focused on two main areas of particular relevance to public libraries:

- working with public libraries and other agencies to widen access to collections and to support lifelong learning
- working with the higher education sector to extend developments in higher education to other sectors.

From the 41 bids submitted to this Call, ten were selected for funding, five of which are being jointly funded with either Resource or RSLP, with two being funded co-operatively by all three funding partners. The BL is a partner in all ten successful projects. As intended, public libraries featured strongly in most of the bids submitted to the Call, as well as in the final list of funded projects. Full details of all the successful projects can be found on the Concord website, at **www.bl.uk/concord/callspro2.html**.

With higher education

The British Library and the higher education sector have a long history of working together, and the BL regards partnership with higher education as a strategic priority. During the last two years there has been an increased emphasis on identifying key areas for further collaboration, with jointly funded studies pointing towards a future in which there will be formal arrangements between the higher education sector, the national libraries and other nationally important collections. These partnerships will implement the development and management of a distributed national collection of research resources, with new agreements to facilitate access.

Close working relationships between the BLCPP and RSLP, which funds initiatives in higher education, have resulted in a number of jointly funded projects and the involvement of the BL in 17 collaborative projects that were successful in bids to RSLP. The RSLP-funded projects included collaborative collection management or collection mapping and resource discovery relating to Asian materials, foreign legal materials, British official publications, company annual reports, materials for Russian and East European studies and research resources for Caribbean studies. Discussions are also underway in the University of London and the M25 Consortium regarding collaboration in collection development of, and access to, research materials in London and the south east. Chapters 5 and 8 address topics of direct relevance to co-operation and funding in higher education.

A recent BL service, *zetoc*, which was launched in September 2000 and further enhanced in 2001, is specifically tailored to the needs of the academic sector, and is available to all further and higher education institutions in the UK. It provides students and academics with desk-top access to the tables of contents of 15 million journal articles from some 20,000 current journals, together with 16,000 conference papers published each year.

In digital programmes

New strategic directions highlighted the web as a key strand of the BL's future strategy. It will enable the Library to become a major player in a variety of collaborative arrangements both nationally and internationally, provide better services in support of scholarship, research and innovation and expand its services to the general public.

The BL has been successful in gaining funding of £3.2 million from the New Opportunities Fund for its *In Place* digitization project, as part of a consortium project led by the Library, entitled *A Sense of Place (National)*. *In Place* will digitize geographical and topographical learning resources relating to places in Britain; resources reflecting diverse aspects of British culture, history and identity; and materials for learners interested in a geographically wider sense of place, drawn from collections relating to several Commonwealth countries. Through the project, high quality learning materials will be created and made accessible through the People's Network and the National Grid for Learning. The Library is also a senior partner in a project led by the Public Record Office, *Moving Here*, with content based on migrations to England.

Among the international partnerships and projects in which the British Library is active is Fathom, which involves the BL, Columbia University in New York, the London School of Economics, Cambridge University Press, the Smithsonian Institution's National Museum of Natural History and the New York Public Library, together with an increasing number of other cultural and educational contributors of international standing. Through its website, Fathom provides a growing range of e-course and related content of high quality. Another example of a collaborative project in which the BL is involved is the International Dunhuang Project (IDP), which promotes research, facilitates preservation and enhances access to a highly significant but scattered and fragile collection of Central Asian manuscripts. Further details of IDP can be found in Chapter 6.

In preservation

Through its own preservation programme and through its support of the National Preservation Office, the BL is involved in a number of collaborative preservation initiatives. In the rapidly changing world of digital preservation, the overall lead in the UK will be taken by the Digital Preservation Coalition (DPC), which will develop a national digital preservation agenda within an international context. The Coalition was developed during 2001 by a small group of partners, led by the UK Joint Information Systems Committee and including the BL, and began operations in the autumn. It was formally incorporated as a limited not-for-profit company in January 2002 and had its launch reception at the House of Commons in February. As part of its remit, the DPC will keep up to date the *Digital materials workbook* (Beagrie and Jones, 2001), which was compiled by people with experience in the field and, with CPP support, subsequently tested in libraries.

The BLCPP also funded a feasibility study for a collaborative approach to mass deacidification as a contribution to the national preservation strategy for the cultural written heritage. Follow-up work has included drawing up a draft tender specification for a mass deacidification facility and undertaking pilot surveys in a number of institutions in London and the south east to determine the level of acid deterioration. More details of these activities together with an overview of current and recent significant collaborative preservation initiatives is provided in Chapter 6.

On the international scene

As the national library of the UK, the British Library has always played a major part in international activities. It is a member of both the Conference of Directors of National Libraries (CDNL), which promotes understanding and co-operation on matters of common interest to national libraries worldwide, and of the Conference of European National Librarians (CENL), which aims to reinforce the role of national libraries in Europe, particularly regarding their responsibilities for maintaining their national cultural heritage and ensuring accessibility of knowledge. The BL has participated in numerous co-operative projects and initiatives, many of them within European Union programmes, such as BIBLINK, and continues to play an important role in projects such as *Bibliotheca Universalis* and The European Library (TEL).

BIBLINK ran from 1996 to 2000, with funding from the European Commission's Telematics Applications Programme. Its aim was to establish a relationship between national bibliographic agencies and publishers of electronic material, in order to create authoritative bibliographic information that would benefit both sectors. It was led by the BL and partners included the national libraries of France, the Netherlands, Norway and Spain.

The main objective of *Bibliotheca Universalis* is to make the major works of the world's scientific and cultural heritage accessible to a wide public via multimedia technologies and to foster the exchange of knowledge and dialogue over national and international borders. The seven founding partners comprised the national libraries of France, Japan, Canada, Italy, the Library of Congress, the Deutsche Bibliothek and the BL. Five new partners have joined, representing Belgium, the Czech Republic, the Netherlands, Portugal, Spain and Switzerland.

The European Library is a 30-month co-operative project funded largely by the European Commission, uniting ten European partners, and combining the resources of a number of Europe's national libraries. Its aim is to make recommendations on how to improve 'interoperability' across national boundaries, against the background of an awareness that, as global networks grow in significance, it is becoming increasingly more important to share knowledge and standards. Chapter 9 explores the international co-operative environment in more detail.

Looking ahead

As the national library of the UK, the British Library is committed to working co-operatively and in partnership with others. This commitment to co-operation has been recognized and welcomed by Resource – the BL's Co-operation and

Partnership Programme is seen as a possible model for other national 'memory' institutions. The BL is building on and enhancing its links with the world of libraries, while at the same time exploring synergies with the museum and archive domains. Technological change gives the BL the opportunity to create valuable new services, which can benefit the whole population, supporting the increasing emphasis within the nation on lifelong learning. On the international scene, new forms of collaborative working are being pursued in order that expertise can be shared, while ambitious projects with which the BL is closely involved, such as The European Library initiative, seek to provide co-ordinated digital collection development plus open and seamless access to digital resources across major European national libraries.

References

Beagrie, N. and Jones, M. (2001) *Preservation management of digital materials workbook: implementation in libraries*, BL Co-operation and Partnership Report 10, available at
www.bl.uk/concord/projec15.html

British Library (1999) *Strategic plan 1999–2002: the outcome of the Library's 1998 strategic review,* London, British Library.

British Library (2001) *New strategic directions*, London, British Library.

Harris, R., Feather, J. and Evans, M. (2000) *The legal deposit of local publications: a case study of Leicestershire, Leicester and Rutland*, Library and Information Commission Research Report 70, London, Library and Information Commission.

2
Mapping the British co-operative landscape

Nick Moore and Julie Carpenter

After many years of financial restraint, and a political climate that was not conducive to public sector innovation and development, life in Britain is changing. The delivery of effective public services has moved up the political agenda and there is growing pressure to find new ways of meeting users' needs. Many libraries have responded by developing new, co-operative arrangements that will enable them to extend the range, or improve the cost-effectiveness, of their services.

Towards the end of 1999, the British Library Co-operation and Partnership Programme (BLCPP) commissioned Education for Change and Acumen to explore the emerging pattern of co-operation. The aim was to produce a broad-brush map of national and regional co-operation between libraries in the UK (Education for Change and Acumen, 2000). We identified 31 library co-operatives that are undertaking work at regional or national level in the five areas of interest to the British Library (BL): collection development, preservation and retention, access, bibliographic services and record creation. The research revealed a vibrant, diverse and dynamic pattern of co-operation. Several co-operatives are well established and have been self-sustaining for over half a century. Alongside these is a similar number set up in the last three years to experiment with, or to develop, new forms of service. It is a rich picture, but one that raises a number of issues that are likely to affect the future development of library co-operation in the UK.

The overall picture

Within the UK there is a broad balance between national and regional activity. Fourteen of the consortia identified were operating at national level while the remaining 17 operated regionally. There is a similar balance between single sector and cross-sectoral co-operation, with cross-sectoral co-operative initiatives being slightly more common. The variation was particularly marked at the regional level where 11 of the 16 consortia were operating cross-sectorally. This suggests that librarians from different sectors are more likely to come into contact with each other in a regional forum than they are nationally.

One striking issue to emerge from the study is the almost total lack of cross-domain co-operation. At national level, only the National Preservation Office (NPO) could be said to be whole-heartedly cross-domain, involving as it does the Public Record Office (PRO), while at the regional level we were only able to identify the AIM25 group (Archives in London and the M25 area) as a cross-domain activity. Given the recently expressed intention of Resource: the Council for Museums, Archives and Libraries to stimulate cross-domain working both nationally and, particularly, within the regions, it would appear that there is considerable scope for development in the years to come.

Turning to the five major areas of co-operation, it is clear that most effort is being devoted to improving users' access to library resources. Twenty-eight of the 31 projects had some form of concern for access, an area that has been the traditional preserve of the regional library systems with their interlibrary lending schemes, union catalogues and transport arrangements. This is now being supplemented by a number of projects seeking to develop better virtual access, either through digital document delivery or through improved provision of library catalogues.

The second most active area was collection development, where, again, the regional library systems accounted for much of the work. For many years they have sought to improve collection development through co-ordinated acquisition schemes of one kind or another, making an impact mainly in the public library sector. The work of these co-operatives is now being supplemented by collection development activity in the academic library sector.

Eleven co-operative initiatives were concerned with the provision of bibliographic services and seven with record creation. Here, the greatly improved national provision of bibliographic information from the British Library and others has, almost certainly, reduced the need for co-operative activity of a generalist kind. There does, however, appear to be a residual need for specialist provision, such as the work for visually impaired people that is being undertaken by Share the Vision. A clear necessity also exists to manage the bibliographical control of digital information resources.

The overall impression given by the map is one of considerable activity, with a high level of innovation and experimentation. There are few obvious gaps, with the notable exception of cross-domain co-operation.

The characteristics of the co-operatives

It is possible to divide the UK's library co-operatives into three categories. First, there is a solid core of well-established consortia, many of which trace their origins back to the 1920s and 1930s. Twelve out of the 31 co-operatives identified had been established before 1990. Eight of these are regional library systems. All these co-operative ventures are self-sustaining. A number make use of external funds to finance development and other activities but their core costs are covered by income raised through charges or members' subscriptions. In the main, their future seems assured – they are performing a range of services that appear to be valued by their members and, in most cases, are actively involved in service development and other improvements.

The second group of five co-operatives is also self-sustaining. These were established during the 1990s, with some originating in development or experimental projects. Three others had what might be thought of as more traditional origins: they resulted from the coming together of a group of like-minded librarians who felt that they could achieve more by working together than they could by working alone. Only when these co-operatives had become established did they begin to attract external funds to enable them to extend the reach of their activities.

The third group, numbering 11 out of the 31 co-operative ventures, is much more recent in origin. They have all been established since 1997 and are at different stages of development; only one appears to be self-sustaining. The remainder are dependent on external, time-limited funds, although the nature of the funding and the dependence varies considerably.

Other projects in this category are bottom-up initiatives, many of which have been developed in response to the existence of some form of external funding. In many cases, these external funds will have covered the initial start-up or development costs, and the resultant co-operative activity will be able to continue at a significantly reduced annual cost. In such circumstances, there is a good chance that the participating organizations will agree to meet their share of the co-operative's costs and the activity will move towards self-sustenance.

Thus, while a relatively high proportion of co-operatives is dependent on external, time-limited funds, this does not necessarily mean that their future is in jeopardy. On the whole, the prospects for continued survival appear to be good. What there may be, however, is a need to develop a range of new funding models upon which such co-operatives can draw instead of having to rely on more conventional, subscription-based models.

Two-thirds of the consortia are actively using information and communication technology to extend the range of their services, or are exploring how they might do so. Not surprisingly, ten of the 11 co-operatives established since 1997 are concerned with technological applications and developments. Equally unsurprising is the fact that seven of the 12 pre-1990 co-operatives were not known to be actively exploring new applications of technology.

International lessons

During the course of the study, we considered a number of co-operative ventures in North America, the Netherlands and Scandinavia, seeking models that might be transferable to the UK. The historical, political and funding circumstances underlying co-operation in the USA are very different in character from those in the UK and we concluded that they did not yield any useful models.

The characteristics of library co-operation in Europe provide more fruitful ground for comparison. We were particularly struck by the relevance of some of the national co-operative developments from the Netherlands, where there is a high degree of national direction and control over co-operation in bibliographic services and user access. Many library collections are accessible via networks in the shared cataloguing system of Pica, the Center for Library Automation and its online information services, operational since 1978. The Dutch Central Catalogue and its interlibrary loan function have been in existence since 1983, first for periodicals and, since 1988, for monographs. In 1999 this system included bibliographic records of the holdings of more than 400 participating libraries.

In the Netherlands, co-operative collection development is highly developed at both national and regional levels. Examples include the Virtual Electronic Library, an initiative for joint core journal collections in economics and business administration between three university libraries, in which Pica also participates; and the Dutch Electronic Subject Service (Dutchess), which is a national system for the retrieval of internet resources relevant to the academic student and research communities. Co-ordinated collection development in academic libraries in the Netherlands ultimately aims to provide, nationally, adequate and fast access to a wide variety of specialized literature within limited budgets. The principle behind it is the strengthening of the national collection through resource sharing and collaboration; activities are funded from existing budgets with no external funding.

Establishing collection and collecting profiles is seen as an important part of co-operative collection development and national co-ordination of collection development requires uniform or at least comparable descriptions of collections in participating libraries. The existing collection strengths and current collecting intensities are being mapped with the Conspectus method and the Dutch Basic Classification, which is also used for shared indexing.

In the area of preservation, the Metamorfoze initiative focuses on the preservation of manuscripts, books, newspapers and periodicals of Dutch origin from the 1840–1950 period in those libraries with a designated preservation function. While these libraries are responsible for the preservation of their collections, a substantial proportion of the costs is subsidized through Metamorfoze.

In these different ways, Dutch librarians have been able to demonstrate the benefits that can accrue from co-operative working, particularly at national level. The UK could well learn useful lessons from the Dutch experience in co-operation.

Key influences, trends and issues

Many significant social, political, infrastructural and technological trends and influences appear to be shaping the emerging map of co-operative initiatives in education, libraries and other cultural heritage sectors.

Overall national influences

Politics will always be an important determinant of the level of co-operation between public sector organizations. Currently, in Britain, the national political climate is more conducive to co-operative initiatives than it has ever been. Since 1997 there have been three major political shifts that serve to stimulate, or to facilitate, co-operation and joint working: regionalism, joined-up government and a willingness to finance change and development.

First among the political influences is regionalism and constitutional change. Despite evident differences between the designated regions, in terms of cultural and social cohesion, equality of service provision and economic power, there is a centrally driven impetus to develop a strategic planning capability at regional level. This will be delivered through the Scottish Parliament, the Welsh and Northern Ireland Assemblies and, in England, through the Regional Development Agencies.

Scotland, Wales and Northern Ireland – as well as some regions in England, such as the North East – are distinguished by a very strong sense of political and social cohesion, and identity as a region. Such cohesion engenders a real culture of co-operation in the planning and provision of all public services. It is difficult, if not impossible, to create social cohesion of this kind. Where it does not exist, new building blocks for a co-operative culture need to be found. At the very least, it is necessary to be able to demonstrate the measurable benefits that will arise from the co-operative activity.

Second, there is now a strong political imperative to collaborate across sectors and domains — the concept of 'joined up government'. This will undoubtedly make it easier for librarians, archivists and museum curators to co-operate and to develop jointly provided services.

The third significant political change is the present government's willingness to finance the process of change and development. In the public library sector, for example, the government has done much to stimulate co-operative working through the provision of challenge funding, while the willingness of funding bodies in the academic sector to use top-sliced resources is making a real impact on the level of co-operative activity. In particular, the attitudes of funding authorities, individual boards and committees towards co-operation enabled by technology have been shaped by the growing public awareness and understanding of the capability of information and communications technology. As a result, technology has become an important enabler, rather than a driver, of co-operation.

International influences on UK co-operative activity have been strong, particularly in the use of technology to deliver new services. In particular, the European Union's (EU) Telematics and Information Society research programmes, which have been operating over the last decade, have made a considerable impact on all public sectors of the library and information system.

Sectoral- and domain-level influences

The expenditure constraints of the 1980s and 1990s made it very difficult for libraries in the UK to finance speculative development or to experiment with novel forms of service. Paradoxically, the very fact that expenditure was constrained increased the need to find new ways of doing things in cost-effective ways. Perhaps one of the biggest changes that has come about in recent years is the growing availability of centrally provided resources that can be used to underwrite the costs of experimentation and development.

The existence of substantial external funding has given libraries a chance to seek out and experiment with innovative ideas and partnerships. Success in winning such funding has provided important building blocks on which to begin development and has led to co-operative partnerships within the library community as well as outside it.

Many of the co-operative activities identified through this mapping study were, in one way or another, supported by external finance; the current high level of innovative development is, in no small part, a result of this new availability of project finance. There is, however, a residual problem associated with long-term funding. In some cases, the co-operative projects have been sustainable, with library managers able to justify absorbing the costs into their recurrent budgets. In other cases the short-term prospects for the co-operative activity after the project funding ends seem bleak, even though there may be reasonable long-term prospects.

Success, of course, tends to generate further success, as the skills of conceiving and preparing successful funding bids are developed within an institution. The danger is that external funding, accessed through project proposal submission, is polarizing the library, archive and museum communities into those with the skills to succeed and those without. There is also a growing danger of initiative overload. Bidding for and managing projects can absorb a disproportionate amount of senior staff time and there seems to be some evidence that libraries are becoming increasingly selective when bidding for funds.

In the public library sector, the impact of local government reorganization of the late 1990s, which increased the number of local authorities in England, is still being felt in the planning, funding and operation of co-operative services. Co-operative arrangements have been developed in order to keep services running at the same levels as before. However, as the new authorities find their feet, they may be as likely to look to demographically similar authorities to share services as to their immediate neighbours; networked technology will make this a real possibility.

Overall, the prospects are very positive. After a long period of financial restraint leading to relatively constrained development we can now identify a range of new opportunities and possibilities. The scope for innovative development is probably greater now than at any time in the past. Admittedly, there are problems associated with sustainability and with achieving a balance between basic service provision and innovation, but the opportunities are there for those who wish to seize them.

Key factors affecting library co-operation

A range of factors – particularly size, sources of funding, control and management – have an impact on co-operative activity.

Critical size

There are two aspects to the size issue. The first concerns the extent and cohesion of geographical areas, the density of the populations served by co-operative programmes, and the location of major service points. Small and dispersed communities are difficult to serve effectively. Users in such communities can call on only a limited range of service providers, which, in turn, are usually unable to benefit from economies of scale. In such circumstances, co-operation is desirable but difficult to achieve. In contrast, people in large conurbations can choose from a range of service providers, each of which is usually able to take advantage of economies of scale. In cases like these, co-operation is less essential but much easier to manage.

The point at which economies of scale can be reached is a crucial one. Libraries are subject to significant scale economies: the larger the library system, the lower the cost of providing an additional unit of service. Thus, the public library authorities that have been reduced in size as a result of local government reorganization have seen their unit costs increase; a number of them are seeking to counter this through co-operation.

There is, however, a paradox here. While small library systems may feel a greater need for co-operation to overcome the limitations imposed by their small size, many of the most successful co-operative schemes are driven by large library systems. This tends to suggest that a certain critical mass is required before libraries are able to contemplate co-operative activity, or, more precisely, to commit a sufficient amount of senior staff time to initiate it.

Co-operative activity based on technology and networking is liberated from many of the constraints imposed by geographical size and the dispersal of populations. As networks become more ubiquitous, they are likely to stimulate new forms of library co-operation, bringing together partners that previously may not have had much contact one with the other.

The second aspect of the size issue relates to the scale of the actual co-operating consortium or partnership. As the number of partners grows, it becomes necessary to establish a central co-ordinating unit that can assume many of the management functions. In due course, this central unit may take over the initiative for developing and extending the range of co-operative activity. Some of the regional library systems provide examples of this and the growth of regionalization is likely to stimulate the trend further.

As well as size, a common culture helps when managing co-operation. Co-operation within a single sector is much more common than cross-sectoral co-operation, and cross-domain co-operation is a rarity.

Sources of funding

Co-operation produces benefits, but it is not without its costs. It is an activity that may result in service improvements, but it will seldom reduce the level of gross expenditure. For libraries, therefore, embarking on co-operation implies making an investment in the expectation of future returns, rather than realizing short-term cost savings. The availability of adequate funds is, therefore, a key factor in determining the nature and extent of co-operation between libraries.

In the traditional model of library co-operation, individual library systems came together to undertake an activity that would result in mutual benefit for the partners. Any costs were met out of the recurrent budgets of the partners with each contributing to a common pool. Increasingly, that model of funding is becoming the exception rather than the rule. Even in the regional library systems, where the traditional model has endured longest, there is now a growing reliance on externally provided funds. Members' subscriptions cover basic costs but service development is financed from project-specific grants coming from a wide range of sources.

The availability of these external sources of funds has undoubtedly been a significant spur to the development of co-operation in recent years – the lack of such funds certainly placed a significant constraint on the development of co-operation in the 1980s and 1990s. In assessing their impact, it is useful to distinguish between funds that are set aside from an overall allocation to a sector – as is the case with the top-sliced funding in the higher education sector – and those funds that genuinely represent an additional financial contribution to the sector. An example here would be the funding designed to support the implementation of the People's Network, which is a project funded by the UK government to create thousands of information and communications technology (ICT) learning centres, based in public libraries, linking all 4300 to the internet.

The top-slicing of higher education funding for initiatives in this sector has provided a spur to co-operation in library and information services, as well as in archives. While higher education funding bodies can choose to opt out of such top-slicing, individual institutions cannot. University libraries have no choice but to buy into, or take part in, many co-operative initiatives, though in some cases their own funding priorities and choices may have been different. There is, therefore, a strong incentive to bid for funds and this has served to increase the overall amount of co-operation taking place.

When funds are top-sliced from an overall allocation, the funding authorities are usually unwilling, if not unable, to support activity outside their sector. While this presents a barrier to cross-sectoral co-operation, there is, however, a strong incentive for libraries to bid for resources that are additional to those allocated to the sector. Whether the funds are top-sliced or represent a real addition to sectoral resources, the availability of external funding is a catalyst to co-operative activity across the library community and is already proving to be so across cultural heritage domains. However, a number of issues for concern emerged from the research. The first is the tendency to encourage short-term thinking. All externally funded projects promote co-operation and partnership in so far as viable project consortia are a prerequisite of success in winning funds, but project consortia tend to be put together swiftly in response to funding opportunities, with none of the careful planning, research into benefits and consultation that is usually the hallmark of successful joint arrangements in the longer-term. In such instances there can be doubts, therefore, about the sustainability of project partnerships after the end of the project.

Sustainability of funding is another cause for concern. Most external funds are time-limited and, once they have dried up, co-operative programmes must look around for further funding. This uncertainty may inhibit effective planning and decision-making. Sources of external funds often require the provision of some level of matching funds from the consortium or bidding partnership – usually a minimum of 10% and sometimes substantially more. This is cited by several library organizations as a barrier to obtaining external funds, particularly at times when core budgets are under pressure. It also serves as a spur to polarization, with the less well-endowed library authorities becoming more disadvantaged. Self-sustainability should, however, continue to be the goal for library co-operatives. This can be achieved in two ways: the traditional approach, that is, reliance on members' subscriptions, is being supplemented more and more by the use of service charges, which help to overcome equity problems between members. There is a general need to develop a better understanding of the dynamics of both subscriptions and charges. Allied to this is a need to explore the implications of a shift to full commercial operation.

The fate of most of the Library and Information Plans (LIPs), which were so actively promoted by the British Library Research and Development Department, indicates the importance of some start-up financing for co-operative activities once the initial planning has been undertaken (Fox, 1998). In many cases, project funds and grants from external sources have filled the gap when library funding authorities are unable or unwilling to do so themselves. However, when the external funds are not available, it has proved difficult to provide the impetus required to transform plans into reality. This is likely to become increasingly important as library co-operation becomes more dependent on technology. There will be a growing need for start-up funding to cover the need for investment in the technological infrastructure.

There is much evidence to suggest that different funding sources, with varying financial decision-making procedures, present major challenges to co-operation across sectors and domains. The library and information community in particular, cutting across statutory public services, basic and higher education, industrial interests, commercial and business interests, and cultural heritage, is characterized by a plethora of funding sources, models and procedures. However, the problem arises with equal force in the archive domain, while museums are polarized between the national museums with central government provision, and local or regional museums funded through local government or the private sector.

This major drawback of the funding initiatives, namely, that they tend to encourage single sector activity at a time when cross-sectoral and cross-domain activity is being encouraged, is the result of the funding bodies' inability to support activity outside their sector.

At the conclusion of the developmental phase of a new co-operative, funds are essential to ease the transition between developmental and full operation. At this point there is a high risk of failure, despite the intrinsic merits of a co-operative scheme, simply because the partners may have been unable to allocate the necessary funds within their annual budgets. Transition funds could do much to overcome this problem. Finally, there is a need for funding to facilitate cross-sectoral and cross-domain work: cross-sectoral approaches are clearly desirable in many circumstances. As the 'joined up' government agenda is pursued, thinking and acting across domains will become imperative.

Control and management structures

The structures for managing and controlling library co-operation have changed significantly in recent years. In part, this is a simple reflection of the increased pressure for accountability and control in the management of public services. It also reflects attempts to overcome the inherent limitations of the basic model of co-operation.

During the last four or five years the impact of public service accountability and Best Value (an initiative spearheaded by the Department for Transport, Local Government and the Regions, involving a performance framework placed on local authorities by central government to encourage them to plan and deliver services according to clear standards of cost and quality) has been significant. The effect has been to tighten up the management of consortia and to focus much more attention on costs and benefits. In the case of new initiatives, more time and effort has been put into researching the potential benefits and drawbacks of co-operation before embarking on the activity. In other cases, the costs and benefits emerge through an externally funded project phase, on the basis of which decisions are made about long-term support.

There is also growing pressure for management structures to be completely clear, with real transparency, whatever the nature of joint arrangements. In practice, partnerships have often arisen without this clarity, frequently building on an existing history of collaboration and an already established shared agenda. The transformation of the Birmingham Libraries Co-operative Mechanisation Project (BLCMP) into Talis Information Ltd is an example of an attempt to introduce greater clarity into a well-established and successful co-operative in order to meet the need for members to demonstrate Best Value in their purchasing decisions.

Models of co-operation

In the traditional model of co-operation, groups of libraries come together to form a consortium to undertake an activity or to provide a joint service. The consortium is usually managed by a committee, either elected by the members or on which each partner has an equal place. The work of the consortium is shared between the members more or less equally and each receives a benefit that they feel is in line with the cost of the contribution made. Many larger co-operative initiatives, such as regional library systems, began life as some form of joint committee or consortium, with a formal body made up of the participating institutions and authorities, but with limited powers and no independent existence. This 'bottom-up' model is robust and appears to have lots of life left in it.

As the scale of the co-operative activity grows, staff are appointed to undertake central tasks. They remain, however, under the control of the members' committee. There is clearly a tension between the control exercised by the committee and the autonomy of the central staff. As the number of members or the size of the central unit grows, the central team begins to assume day-to-day responsibility for the work of the co-operative, with the committee setting overall policy. Another point that can affect the balance of power between the committee and the staff is the use of external project-specific funds. In some of the regional library systems, there has been a steady increase in project-specific income relative to members' subscriptions and, in these cases, it is possible to identify a strengthening in the position of the consortium's staff.

There are several limitations inherent in this model. The principle of mutual benefit means that it is difficult to undertake activities that might benefit some more than others. This raises the question of how each institution perceives benefit in the context of the initiative, and how each weighs up the balance between institutional costs and benefits. More particularly, it tends to limit the co-operative to the provision of relatively low-level generalist services. It also makes it difficult to undertake cross-sectoral activities or even to attract members from different sectors. A number of the regional library systems have sought to overcome this through such developments as flexible subscription arrangements, but the essential limitation remains. Nevertheless, this traditional model is quite robust. Many of the co-operative schemes that have been established in the academic library sector through top-sliced funding initiatives, for example, are structured in this way. It is cheap, easily understood, flexible and can be established quickly.

An alternative model that has emerged in recent years is what might be termed the 'centre plus hubs' model. This structure is common to a number of the co-operative arrangements brought about as a result of a top-down initiative. An example of this is the Resource Discovery Network (RDN), which is a co-operative network consisting of a central organization, the Resource Discovery Network Centre, and a number of independent subject-focused service providers called hubs. This model is particularly common in the higher education sector, no doubt resulting from the use of top-sliced resources to promote development initiatives. The advantage for the funder is that it provides a single administrative, lead organization working with a number of secondary units to which it delegates different functions. Lines of management responsibility are transparent and are frequently determined by contract or service-level agreement. The model thus avoids many of the limitations of management by committee. It is also easier to control imbalances between costs and benefits, as contributions from the hubs are usually made under contract in return for an agreed fee.

Another approach is to establish a commercial operation to manage the consortium and provide services to members. The London and South-East Library Region (LASER) and BLCMP, among others, set up arms-length companies or agencies to overcome the other structural limitations of the traditional model. While still fairly new and therefore relatively untested, this appears to be a sustainable model with potential applications in all sectors. It is not, however, without drawbacks and these need to be taken fully into account when establishing the company. There are, for example, major questions of ownership. Do members of the co-operative venture have the right to sell their share if they decide to leave the company? There is also the question of profit and how it is to be distributed. The model does, however, open up interesting scope for co-operative ventures to provide services to a wider client and service base in order to respond to user needs within the prevailing economic and political climate. This model also potentially provides a means of overcoming the need for heavy investment in research and product development, as the company could raise investment capital on commercial terms.

Service agency agreements, which are a long-established form of operation in local government, are another model of co-operation with particular potential for local as distinct from regional or national situations. They are a variation on contracting out, in which the contract to provide the service or services is placed with one local authority by a client authority, which retains formal responsibility for the services. While outside the scope of this study, they provide a model that has considerable future potential for local co-operative ventures.

A new co-ordinated development model of co-operation has emerged in recent years, notably in the higher education sector, as the result of top-down initiatives in which funding bodies set out programmes designed to achieve certain specified strategic aims. Such programmes are backed by significant financial resources, which are often top-sliced from national allocations, and usually involve a competitive bidding process, thus providing scope for initiatives from below within a top-down programme. This approach appears to be very effective and has certainly stimulated a considerable amount of co-operative activity in recent years, encouraging a number of innovative approaches to service development.

One or two commercial models of co-operation are beginning to appear, as a direct response to the need for clearer lines of management and accountability, together with greater transparency between purchasers and providers. These commercial models offer considerable potential for future application; in particular they provide a means of raising investment capital to finance expenditure on technological development and the creation of a networked infrastructure.

Whatever the structural model chosen for the co-operative entity, all partners must give up some autonomy and control, limiting their freedom to move. This sets limits to co-operation and can be a barrier for senior managers, funding authorities and other stakeholders, particularly when embarking on new co-operative ventures. Once again this emphasizes the importance of being able to assess the balance of benefits against costs.

Conclusions

Our general conclusion is that co-operation is alive and well in the UK. The long tradition of co-operation within the library community seems set to continue into the future, being refreshed along the way by new approaches, new forms and structures and, in particular, new applications of information and communication technology. Co-operation will continue to be seen by service providers and their funders as a cost-effective way of achieving improvements in the scale and quality of the services offered.

The overall picture

There is a core of well-established, self-sustainable library co-operatives operating at national and regional level, many of which have been in existence for over 50 years and which are adapting effectively to changing technologies, political circumstances and service requirements. This core is being supplemented by a significant group of new co-operative initiatives that are exploring new issues and new applications of technology. While most of these new co-operatives are currently dependent on time-limited external funds, there are good prospects for self-sustainability.

Library co-operation continues to be driven by a desire for mutual benefit, achieved by extending the range or quality of services offered by the libraries to their users. There is little evidence to suggest that libraries now join together as a means of surviving hard times; rather, co-operation seems to flourish in a time of optimism and expansion.

New structures and ways of operating for library co-operatives are emerging in response to wide-ranging political changes. There is a perceived need for greater transparency and for a more accurate quantification of costs and benefits.

Especially at regional level, there is a growing trend towards cross-sectoral work. The increased influence of external funding, however, inhibits the degree of cross-sectoral and cross-domain activity, as most of the funds are restricted to use within a single sector of the library community. A notable exception is the fund administered by the BLCPP, which aims to be cross-sectoral and cross-domain.

There is currently a significant lack of cross-domain activity at both national and regional level. This lack is likely to be felt keenly and become more apparent in the coming years as Resource pursues its aim of increasing cross-domain working, particularly at the regional level. The pursuit of this objective will, however, almost certainly open up new opportunities for co-operative activity.

The future

Co-operation will continue to be a powerful means of meeting service objectives in a cost-effective way. Libraries and other cultural memory institutions will be able to extend the range and quality of their services by sharing costs and so taking advantage of scale economies, by avoiding duplication of effort and by improving virtual and physical access to regional and national library and information resources. In so doing, they will be assisted by more use of external funds to stimulate development. This will increase the scope for co-operative activity but it will bring with it a requirement to develop skills in managing projects, services and co-operative endeavour within a bidding culture, and to develop flexible models for co-operation.

The coming years will see a continuation of the steadily decreasing importance of conventional interlibrary lending – the past driver of much co-operation. This will be a consequence of the continuing influence of the British Library Document Supply Centre (BLDSC), allied to more general moves towards digital document delivery. Both these factors will emphasize national and international solutions rather than regional ones and this will lead to a reduced interlibrary lending role for the regional library systems (RLSs). Many have already responded positively to this trend and are actively developing new suites of services for their members; one responded by announcing its intention to disband.

It is, however, important to recognize that there is a corresponding growth in the political importance of the English regions as well as the devolved administrations in Northern Ireland, Scotland and Wales. This enhanced regional dimension will be beneficial for cross-sectoral activity as it appears to be easier to organize cross-sectoral affairs at regional level than at national. It will probably also be advantageous for cross-domain working.

The last few years have seen the growing importance of technology and, particularly, networking in shaping the nature of library co-operation. It has had a significant impact already and this is likely to grow as networks mature, increasing the scope for co-operation. In their turn, however, new issues will be raised, such as the need to resolve problems of interoperability.

The prospects for future development, therefore, look positive. The foundations are secure, there is no shortage of ideas, creativity or innovation, nor is there any lack of opportunities.

References

Education for Change and Acumen (2000) *Mutual benefit: a map of the co-operative landscape*, a study undertaken for the British Library Co-operation and Partnership Programme, BL Co-operation and Partnership Report 4, available at **www.bl.uk/concord/mapping/mappage.html**

Fox, N. (1998) Library and Information Plans: an enduring concept, *LINC – Issues in Focus*, **15**, (December), 1–4.

3

The view from Resource

Vivien Griffiths and Neville Mackay

The vision

Imagine it is the year 2010. You have had a hard day and you are looking forward to a quiet evening at home. The day started off badly because you had to go into the office for a meeting – very much a rarity at a time when broadband communications and teleconferencing allow most people to work from home. It became worse when your train was delayed – some things, it seems, never change. Far from being greeted by the oasis of tranquillity you expected, you arrive at your front door to be confronted by a hubbub of noise and activity.

Your youngest daughter has occupied the dining room table and is working furiously to complete a homework assignment – homework now being more important than ever since the introduction of the 'living to learn' principle across the entire national curriculum. In the lounge, her brother has monopolized the digital television to find out more about the programme he has seen on dinosaurs on the Discovery Channel.

Your partner is nowhere to be seen. An e-mail on the family bulletin board tells you he has gone out to work on an assignment in support of a course of self-directed learning. He prefers to work at the local library because he likes the buzz and the space, and there are always plenty of friendly staff and other learners around to talk to. Walking through to the kitchen in the vain hope of finding dinner you discover a grandparent working online, digging out some background material for a proposed demonstration against a road development that will cut across a local historic site. In the study your eldest daughter is hunched over your old-fashioned laptop conducting an earnest video link discussion with an aged professor of geography on a culture online site.

All of them are using museum, library and archive services, in their real and virtual forms, to help them with their tasks. All of them have bridged the digital divide and are fully fledged grown up members of the e-society, surfing confidently down the information superhighway towards the digitally enhanced sunset. And for all of them it is as natural and easy a process as breathing or eating.

The challenge

Whether this paints a picture of an utopian ideal or of a dystopian nightmare is perhaps more a matter of individual preference than of verifiable fact. But the scenario is not as far-fetched as it might at first appear. At the time of writing, just over 40% of households in the UK have personal access to the internet, and around half of the country's public library service points offer access to the world wide web. The UK is ahead of every other country in the European Union (EU) on almost any indicator of IT use and access you choose. A plethora of government-funded 'content driven' IT services have sprung up – the People's Network and the National Grid for Learning are just two examples. Notwithstanding this progress, the creative and intelligent use of electronic services in this way is still very much in its infancy, and the way in which organizations provide them is evolving rapidly. There are still enormous challenges to be overcome in order to bring the vision described above alive. What, then, needs to happen to make sure that museum, library and archive services become as central to the lives of ordinary people as this scenario suggests?

There are at least three priorities. First, the services provided by knowledge provision organizations such as libraries, museums and archives need to become truly user-focused. Librarians understand that it would be dangerous to bask in the afterglow of deserved public recognition of their role in community life and appreciation of the service they provide. Even though 60% of the population are members of a public library, and libraries often come top of local authority customer satisfaction surveys, librarians suspect that many members of the public base their judgement on what they are used to, rather than on what they have a right to expect. Librarians realize that they need to know how high, or low, the public's expectations are. And what about the 40% of the population who are not part of the public library family? Why do they not belong? What can be done to make libraries relevant and meaningful places for them? There is an urgent need for less second guessing about what libraries think people want, and more evidence-based research into customer need, not just among those who use libraries but, more importantly, among those who do not. Well researched information about customer needs and expectations is the basis for professional business planning in all organizations. The best library plans are based on evidence gathered from regular use of the data collected by the Public Library User Survey (PLUS) and Children's PLUS. These broad-brush statistics are then fleshed out with smaller-scale, focused research within specific sectors of the community or geographically based areas.

Second, services must be delivered in a truly seamless way so that the user is unaware of their source, whether they are coming from a library, an archive, a university, a museum, from down the road or from Timbuctoo. How often have we all turned disappointed customers away because what they want is somewhere else? Worse still, how often do we hide the fact that frequently we do not know where that somewhere else is? Seamless service delivery is not just an ideal concept – it is a prerequisite for modern library services. Failure to deliver knowledge and information seriously negates the very purpose for which libraries exist.

Finally, library services need to be deliverable in a variety of different media and in a form that the user requires – real, virtual, or both. The user must have that choice. We must not let ill-informed and arcane debates in the media about the role of the book as opposed to the computer obscure the need for both. Information is equally valuable whether it is communicated on paper, digitally, on file, on films, or by word of mouth. The unique skill of librarians is in pulling all these various resources together in a way that helps the user meet his or her particular need.

Now we come to the heart of the matter: none of these challenges can be met without the creation of effective partnership arrangements between libraries and other information and knowledge providers. Crucially, those partnerships should not just be with other libraries, but with a whole range of organizations and individuals across society as a whole – in the cultural sector, in education, in business, in health – in short, with anyone or anything with information and knowledge in which the public has a demonstrable interest.

Partnership is much more than a political buzzword with a flavour of the month feel. It is the path by which libraries can stake their claim to their future – as the street corner university, the idea store or the one-stop shop. The titles do not matter. They will be forgotten long before the memory of the quality of the service they provide fades. Partnerships are an enabling mechanism, allowing libraries 'to boldly go' where none has gone before.

Let us consider the arguments in favour of partnerships and start with the needs of users. Users do not care where information comes from. Users simply want access to the best possible information meeting their particular needs as quickly as possible. In an age when user expectations are being increasingly raised, where media hype and political spin are helping to create a more demanding and sophisticated breed of customers, partnerships are a logical way of improving the range and quality of services that users increasingly expect.

The development of relatively accessible and user-friendly technologies such as the internet has helped to fuel this change in user expectations. However, technology does not merely create opportunities for partnership; it creates an imperative for them, in order to overcome the barriers to access, which it can present when we fail to allow it to work across traditional boundaries. The forms of co-ordination between and across library sectors, which are depicted in the Library and Information Commission's (LIC) report *Empowering the learning community* (2000), demonstrate that partnership working can bring immediate benefits.

This imperative is further reinforced by a growing political momentum at both national and local level. The drive to modernize public services; the focus on e-commerce; the development of joined up government; the implementation of one-stop shops within local authorities; the development of service planning initiatives; Best Value – all of these depend on partnership and all raise the stakes for libraries in staying ahead of the game in what is becoming an increasingly competitive environment.

Finally, consider the extent to which the need to secure funding for the maintenance and delivery of new library services is dependent upon partnership. The nature of libraries and the way in which libraries and other local authority services are funded has changed fundamentally over the past five years. The provision of adequate core funding is still the bedrock on which most public library services are built, but their ability to develop truly exceptional and innovative services is increasingly dependent upon their ability to attract funding from other sources – from central government, from elsewhere within the local authority, from the lottery, or from Europe. The extent to which the development of this 'bidding culture' is a good or bad thing is largely a matter of opinion, but it cannot be ignored as a feature to which libraries must respond in order to remain competitive in the public services provision marketplace.

All of these nettles need to be grasped if libraries, museums and archives are to continue to touch the lives of ordinary people and remain as relevant in the 21st century as they have been in the past. People have less and less spare time and there is an ever-increasing range of alternative and competing activities on offer. There is a change in the expectations of and demands on libraries and the People's Network is only one of the ways in which we need to address that change. Libraries have remarkably loyal customers, but increasingly we need to respond to them in all facets of their lives, as parents, as lifelong learners, as imaginative and adventurous readers, as engaged citizens, as potential community leaders and sometimes as excluded and deprived individuals who need to re-engage with their history, their culture and their community.

What needs to be done?

In its action plan for public libraries, *Building on success* (Resource, 2001a), Resource clearly lays out its commitment to developing and sustaining library services, helping to improve access, focusing on service planning, development and quality assurance and, in particular, emphasizing the need for capacity building and co-operation. Partnership is part of the very fabric of Resource's creation, bringing together the Library and Information Commission (LIC) and the Museums and Galleries Commission (MGC) to promote cross-domain working where shared experience and development opportunities can bring most benefit to services and customers. Regional co-operation is high on Resource's agenda, but other forms of partnership are also highlighted, including arm's length arrangements, with other organizations, trusts, public–private partnerships and Private Finance Initiative (PFI) projects.

Resource sees the huge significance of technology in this scenario. It underpins everything. Libraries, museums and archives cannot expect to be part of the brave new information-driven world unless they wholeheartedly embrace technology. Technology is not a 'bolt on' service, nor is it an end in itself – in essence it is simply a tool that enables the more effective delivery of services. However, it is the scale and nature of the opportunities this creates that are truly breathtaking.

The People's Network project, which will ensure that all the UK's public libraries are connected to the world wide web by 2002, is a major step in this direction, but there is still much more to be done. The initial investment in hardware and people needs to be sustained once the initial three-year funding package expires; the People's Network has to develop in a way that integrates it with other initiatives throughout the public sector, particularly in the fields of education and e-commerce; it needs to expand to embrace museums and archives; and more compelling and accessible content in a full range of media must be created – building upon the momentum generated by the New Opportunities Fund's £50 million digitization programme, linking into other related initiatives in the higher education sector, and capitalizing on the government's proposed Culture and Education Online initiatives. Sustainability and the continuous development of the People's Network are crucial issues for Resource and, together with the creation of high quality content, they are issues that need to be addressed through core funding, not dependent on the vagaries of the bidding culture.

However, more technology is not the complete answer. Libraries must also play to their traditional strengths, providing mediated access to a range of information services with a core service built around print-based resources. Even here, a number of fundamental changes can be seen. We have witnessed a gradual combination of the traditional role of the librarian as a non-judgemental information navigator with that of a skilled and authoritative mediator. We have experienced the growth of overtly educationally driven services, such as reading and homework clubs, and observed greater integration of public library services with other local authority activities and functions.

We also need a library profession willing and able to exploit these opportunities and trends to the utmost. To make this happen we have to develop an even more sophisticated culture of collaboration. Museum, library and archive services must continue to work together. So the final prerequisite – and probably the most difficult of all to achieve – is a change of mindset. Collaboration must be embedded in the warp and weft of daily life. The best museum, library and archive services must have a 'can do' culture, embrace the outreach and access opportunities offered by new technology and rise to the challenges of a society open 24 hours a day, seven days a week. Changing this scenario requires effort by governing bodies, management, staff, recruiters and professional educators and trainers. It is not easy but it can be achieved, and the best of the current services can show the way.

Building on success

Building on success reflects Resource's commitment to support public libraries in fulfilling their full potential in the future and outlines key priorities under four headings:

- developing and sustaining new services
- access to services
- service planning, development and quality assurance
- capacity building and co-operation.

These four areas offer fertile ground for partnership working and there are many excellent examples of imaginative approaches which have been developed over recent years.

Developing and sustaining new services

The case has already been made that libraries, like all organizations, need to change and evolve, developing innovative approaches to service delivery. The impact of new technology and concerns about the future sustainability of the People's Network have led many library services to look for ways of sharing their future development plans and the creation of new services with other partners. Encouragingly, for Resource, many of these partnerships have been formed across libraries, museums and archives services and a good example is the Naval Tradition project in Plymouth.

In December 2000 Plymouth Library Service won over £30,000 from the Department for Culture, Media and Sport (DCMS) Wolfson British History Challenge Fund for a project designed to build up its collection on 'the social and economic impact of the navy and the dockyard on the city of Plymouth and the consequent development of the communities directly affected by them'. Social inclusion is an important aspect of the project. The decline of the dockyard has led to high unemployment, creating two of the most deprived wards in the country. Many special initiatives are seeking to alleviate the resulting social and economic problems, including Health and Education Action Zones, and Single Regeneration Budget funding; the Wolfson project aims to support and complement these where possible.

There was already an established tradition of co-operation between the library service, the City Museum and the Plymouth and West Devon Record Office, and this has been developed as a result of the Wolfson project. A steering group, led by the library service and consisting of representatives from all three organizations, manages the project, with each being responsible for aspects of the work most appropriate to its areas of expertise.

The library has established contact with a large number of individuals and local institutions, encouraging participation in the project. It has conducted a literature search to establish the existence of resources that should be added to the collection and a series of fact sheets on topics relating to the area has been produced, aimed at both secondary school students and at the general public. Eventually it is hoped that this information will be put on the internet through the Plymouth Grid for Learning and included in a teaching pack to be offered to schools. In addition, an index to the naval graves at the No Place Field cemetery has been produced.

The projects being organized by the City Museum are the compilation of a resource directory, bringing together information about relevant records from as many collections as possible, and an oral history project about the working lives of men living in Devonport. Staff from the museum are also participating in a number of complementary projects in the area including a community arts project connected with the redevelopment of the Cannon and Cornwall Streets area. Staff at the Record Office will become involved in the project by contributing to the resource directory and, possibly, by microfilming some of their documents to make them more accessible. A graphic designer is employed jointly by all three organizations and has been invaluable in designing publicity material and fact sheets. Later in the year she will also play an important role in designing the proposed community exhibition, based on information collected during the project, which will tour a number of local venues.

Marketing of the Wolfson project has been co-ordinated jointly. Individuals from the three organizations responsible for it have, collectively, an impressive list of contacts, both nationally and locally, and have undertaken to keep everyone informed of developments as well as encouraging active participation. In March the annual Local Studies Forum was hosted jointly; over 100 members of the public attended this event. This has resulted in several promises of donations of material as well as offers of practical help, ensuring that the project is truly 'owned' by the community.

In Buckinghamshire, a potential catastrophe has led to some innovative cross-sectoral working and a very positive outcome. The disastrous fire at Norwich Library in East Anglia, in which the entire local studies collection was destroyed, prompted a radical review of unique material housed at Buckinghamshire's Local Studies Library, which is located in a similar open plan building of the 1960s. The collection of 10,000 photographs of Buckinghamshire was recognized as particularly vulnerable and plans were made for its transfer to more secure accommodation at the County Museum Technical Centre. In order to preserve public access to the photographs, it was decided to scan the whole collection onto a digital database, which could be made available at service points around the county.

Staff at the County Museum were already scanning their own photographs and prints so that they could be accessed electronically as part of social history displays. The same system was adopted in the library, the images scanned at a modest 100 dpi (dots per inch) using the 'Photostyler' programme for image manipulation, and the photographs themselves catalogued on a MODES database produced by the **mda** (formerly the Museum Documentation Association). The use of common equipment and software enabled the library and museum to merge their databases and to provide public common access to their combined collection of about 25,000 images, either on sets of CD-ROMs or on the library's own network. Every effort was made to contact the copyright owners of images less than 70 years old and only one individual declined to have his material scanned into the system.

The work of scanning and cataloguing the photographs was completed in 1997, just at the time when the Local Studies Library merged with the County Record Office to form the Buckinghamshire Records and Local Studies Service. The plan to move the original photographs to the Museum Technical Centre was reviewed and it was decided to locate all the photographs, from both the library and the museum collections, in the fireproof strongrooms of the County Record Office. All three of Buckinghamshire's heritage services were now involved in the project. When the County Council's own IT section was invited to join the project team, the plan to circulate the images and data via CD-ROMs was abandoned and the whole database moved to the County Council website. The database was launched on the internet in March 2000 and currently attracts about 1000 hits per day from visitors from all over the world.

Internet users can log on to the County Council's website at **www.buckscc.gov.uk/** and find '20,000 photographs of Buckinghamshire' either on the 'What's New' page or via the County Records and Local Studies Service home page. Searching is by parish, date, name, or any keyword. Images can be printed for private research, but the site advises anyone wishing to use an image in any publication to contact the Buckinghamshire Records and Local Studies Service.

A new 'Centre for Buckinghamshire Studies', funded by the Heritage Lottery Fund (HLF), incorporating the County Record Office and the Local Studies Library, opened in the autumn of 2001. Work is progressing with the County Museum to add Buckinghamshire prints and works of art to the website, and with the archaeologists in the Planning Department to include data from the Sites and Monuments Records.

Access to services

Empowering the learning community, the LIC report produced in March 2000, pointed up the crucial need for co-operation between libraries in the local authority and education sectors to improve access to resources and expressed disappointment at the dearth of good practice in this area:

> Co-ordination between public libraries, on the one hand, and school or academic libraries, on the other, is inadequate – with rare but important exceptions. This means we are wasting opportunities to achieve more efficient investment in acquisitions, to offer better library support to children and to improve the material and assistance available to lifelong learners.
>
> (Library and Information Commission, 2000, 2)

There are exceptions to that situation and increasingly librarians from all sectors are seeing the sense of joint working. The British Library Co-operation and Partnership Programme (BLCPP) aims to support that good practice and to help libraries to embed it into mainstream service delivery. Resource is supporting this

Programme because it wishes to take this model of collaboration still further, so that it encompasses museums and archives as well as libraries. Examples of existing partnerships include Milton Keynes Learning City Libraries Network, Birmingham Public and Academic Library Services and Lancashire County Council's Learning Centres.

Staff from libraries within Milton Keynes have been meeting and talking together for some time. More recently, discussions have centred on the need for even closer co-operation in line with current thinking about service efficiency, Best Value and the benefits of opening up services to the community. In Milton Keynes and the surrounding region are a number of important libraries: in particular those of the Open University, De Montfort University, Cranfield University, Buckingham University and the General NHS Trust, as well as the public library network run by the Council. Between them, these facilities possess a wide range of information sources and other specialist material supported by knowledgeable staff. In the main, these collections are used by those on campus or those registered with a local public library.

Although some informal referral arrangements have existed, the wider community actually has little knowledge of the substantial resources that are available to them and the creation of a formal network is aimed at breaking down barriers and publicizing the facilities that can be accessed through the scheme. The participating libraries have jointly produced a leaflet, which has been widely distributed and now forms part of the introductory pack given to new borrowers who join the libraries. This provides much clearer information and an outline of how the scheme works. It is a simple system, which a few questions or a telephone call will explain, and only requires a current library membership card to open many doors. For those without a card, joining is usually a straightforward procedure.

This scheme, which was recently launched by the local Member of Parliament, is just a start. There have already been discussions about developing common access to catalogues via Z39.50 technology, and more joint training initiatives, particularly for staff who may need to refer customers on to other scheme members. Over time, it is hoped that some of the restrictions that are placed upon information sources through licensing may be reduced via a joint approach to purchasing, which could help us all whether through cost savings or just by offering wider access to information for everyone. The website at **www.mklclibraries.org/** is maintained by Cranfield University and provides a basic guide to the scheme. It is already linked to the main sites of the participating libraries and will expand to explain new initiatives as they are developed.

PALS – Public and Academic Library Services – was set up in 1991 to explore strategic connections and to promote better practice in service delivery to the many users who frequented both Birmingham Central Library and their own university library. The Universities of Aston, Birmingham and Central England worked with the Central Library and with the library school at UCE (University of Central England) to create better mutual understanding of the context in which learning and library services were offered in Birmingham. Towards the end of PALS' life in 1998, the Orchard Centre and the Universities of Coventry, Warwick and Wolverhampton became members; it was at this point that the growing regional agenda led to the transformation of PALS, as the co-operative process began to shape what would eventually become The Libraries Partnership – West Midlands (TLP–WM).

PALS considered and influenced the following aspects of library services delivery in the city and the region:

1 Access to services, contributing significantly to a lowering of barriers and a reduction in competition: PALS contributed to the influential research project, *People Flows*, conducted by UCE (Nankivell, Foster and Elkin, 2000), which examined cross-sectoral use of libraries in Birmingham, Solihull and Sheffield.

2 The emerging telematics agenda: in 1997 the first Regional Telematics Conference, a deliberately public library affair, led directly to the creation of the post of regional telematics officer; subsequent conferences have been equally deliberately cross-sectoral, and the post itself has now been transformed from a short-term project footing into two development manager posts funded by subscription of all members of TLP–WM.

3 Joint training initiatives, including exchange of experience between the public library and the library school at UCE.

4 Special collections and content development: the University of Birmingham and the Central Library, in particular, hold major collections of regional and national importance. Early discussion about co-operation in a predominantly print-based environment led eventually to the development of *Futures Together*, a regionally based project to map the content of all special collections in libraries (Warren and Dodd, 2000). The report also explores new protocols on access across the different sectors. In turn this solid foundation has enabled web-based projects as diverse as Touchstone (a resource for Shakespeare studies, funded by BLCPP), Revelation (19th- and 20th-century church history and Christian theology resources, funded by RSLP) and the Sense of Place Consortium awarded funding in 2001 by the NOF-digitize initiative.

39

PALS was one of the keystones that brought into life TLP–WM, though this was influenced by other co-operative agendas and the Government's own programme for regionalism. TLP–WM has successfully positioned itself at the core of the regional agenda for libraries; it can claim project-based success with regional, national and European awards, an honest broker status with libraries across all sectors in the region, and recognition through representation at regional cultural and ICT consortia.

Of course co-operation is a constantly shifting process. A new cultural programme has brought new challenges for partnership and networking, and TLP–WM is now responding to a wider regional agenda, which includes museums and archives, and is building toward the establishment of a regional council, which will embrace all three cultural sectors.

An excellent example of partnership between public libraries and the education sector is the establishment of 14 learning centres in public libraries in Lancashire over the last 18 months. Most of these were set up in partnership with local colleges; they are in rural, semi-urban and urban areas and all have proved highly successful, averaging 9000 users per month, across all age ranges. One example of their success is in Preston: when this centre opened there were 2000 drop-in users in the first three months and 400 of those signed up for learning through the college. A second example relates to a partnership with Runshaw College where 12 centres were opened in a range of locations including small libraries, a care home for the elderly, the Leyland Daf Trucks Plant and four other venues. This attracted European Social Fund (ESF) support and North West Agency Skills Development funding to the tune of over £400,000.

A project with the BBC to launch a Learning and Mobile Zone with public libraries, colleges, the County Council's Lifelong Learning Division and the BBC, with the personal support of its director general, has been extremely successful. The Mobile Zone is a specially adapted single decker bus visiting local communities all over Lancashire. The two-year scheme is staffed by a BBC Radio presenter and the bus is equipped with laptops for public use. Radio programmes are broadcast from it daily. This is an exciting development in partnership with the BBC and is a pilot for what is hoped may become a national scheme.

Access to learning opportunities is a fundamental aspect of government policy, but alongside it sits a commitment to social inclusion on a broader front. Public libraries are important to this agenda, because they sit firmly within their local communities and provide access to information and knowledge for excluded people. Some parts of our community are doubly disadvantaged, by a combination of physical or learning impairment, poverty, and social exclusion, which can take many forms.

Resource's commitment to people with sensory impairment has been demonstrated by its support to Share the Vision, which aims to develop library services to people with visual impairment. The recent best practice manual (Resource, 2001b), produced by Share the Vision, has been made available to all library authorities and there are many examples of good practice in it. One that attempts to tackle exclusion created by language barriers, as well as visual impairment, is the Talking Eyes project in Birmingham.

The Talking Eyes service is jointly managed by Birmingham Libraries and Birmingham Focus, a long established voluntary organization working in the field of visual impairment. The current range of services includes a monthly magazine-style community information tape, a consumer issues tape three times per year and a six-monthly topic tape, where a subject is given more in-depth treatment. All tapes are produced in Bengali, Urdu, Gujerati, Hindi and Punjabi and are sent out to blind and partially sighted customers, in the appropriate language. The consumer-issues tape and longer topic-based tapes are produced in English, as well as the five community languages. As a result of a grant from Resource, and in conjunction with Share the Vision, copies of the tapes and publicity material, in each language and in English, have been distributed to library services nationally.

Social exclusion can also manifest itself in the loss of a sense of shared cultural heritage. In Brent, the Black History Month project aims to overcome that loss by celebrating the history of our most recent communities, in partnership with other local stakeholders. Each October, Brent runs London's largest Black History Month programme. This is jointly planned and managed by the library service and by the museum, archive and arts service. Its focus is the celebration of Black history, especially the history of Black people in Brent, and on the promotion of Black literature. In 2000, other partners were also involved, for the first time, in staging events, including the Tricycle Theatre, the adult and community education service, Stonebridge Housing Action Trust, and the College of North West London. There were over 60 events in libraries, the museum, the archive and other venues, including storytelling, readings by prominent Black writers, talks on a range of historical topics, arts and craft workshops, and a popular exhibition on the history of Black footballers. Black History Month was also a platform for the launch of Black Inc., a DCMS Wolfson-funded reader development project, aimed at encouraging new Black writing. Over 2500 people attended events, and there was an equally successful Black History Month in October 2001.

Service planning, development and quality assurance

All public sector bodies are subject to external scrutiny and evaluation, quality assurance processes and a benchmarking approach to service planning. Therefore, a shared approach to setting future priorities can provide better co-ordination of services and help in assessing effectiveness across the board. There are some excellent examples of joint information gathering and subsequent service planning at local and, increasingly, at regional level.

One example is Shropshire Access to Information for Learning (SAIL), which is the lifelong learning sub-group of Shropshire Access to Information Resources (SHAIR), a cross-sectoral planning partnership, including further and higher education institutions, schools, museums, archives, the careers service and Chamber of Commerce, together with the public library service. In addition to the entitlement to use the resources of all the member organizations, SAIL has conducted an audit to find out details of charges, conditions of loan, and access to electronic resources, in order to provide guidelines and encourage wide use from all parts of the local community.

In Sunderland, the Libraries Access Sunderland Scheme (LASh), which offers access to all libraries in the city for anyone who lives, works or studies there, including free internet access and e-mail, has produced a directory of services, available on its website, and has negotiated a city-wide licence for the EBSCO Masterfile service, which gives access to a huge number of full-text electronic periodicals on all libraries' internet terminals.

In several parts of the country, such as the Co-East area, the West Midlands (The Library Partnership) and in Sheffield, as represented by the Sheffield Information Organization (SINTO), various forms of collaboration are in place to improve co-operative service development, seek funding opportunities, support universal access and develop methods of impact assessment. In York, there is an example of joint procurement of a new online library system. A partnership has just been agreed between the City of York Council and the College of Ripon and York St John to share a library computer system. By joining together, York's public libraries and the College have been able to purchase a state-of-the-art library system, which will deliver a highly sophisticated suite of services. The new user-friendly system went live during 2001; it will enable customers and students to search the catalogue, reserve and renew books, both at the library and at home via the internet. Using a special website called 'iBistro', readers will be able to select their favourite titles and be e-mailed when they arrive in the library. For public library users there will also be a telephone renewals system so that customers are not kept waiting when they want to renew their books. College users will have many new and improved services including integrated access to electronic information sources and computer-based requests for books from inside and outside the library.

The college and the public library service will run their systems separately, but the system will be supported by the Council's IT department and customers will benefit from a shared library catalogue. The system has cost £190,000 but both partners have been able to achieve significant savings by sharing the costs. Both libraries hope this will be the first of a number of co-operative ventures.

Capacity building and co-operation

The traditional interlending function, at a regional level, has proved a good platform for more creative regional co-operation at a strategic level. Many former regional library services have developed into organizations well on their way to fulfilling Resource's ambitions for a strong, cross-domain regional body to be in place by 2004. In addition to the learning opportunities to be gained from confident cross-domain working, the libraries, museums and archives sector has the opportunity to position itself more effectively in negotiating with other regional and sub-regional bodies. There are opportunities to be seized in relation to networking developments and to argue for the strengthening of regional library collections together with alternative funding regimes.

Some regional development agencies are a long way down the road of creating a cross-domain and cross-sectoral body. Information North has a long history of co-operation, including all the public library authorities, five university libraries, 24 college libraries and other members from industrial and society libraries. In February 2000 it transformed itself into the North East Museums, Libraries and Archives Council (NEMLAC) and has taken on roles such as approaches to external funding, advice, information and training, best practice and Best Value, flagship projects, grant-making, marketing and promotion, research and development, and strategic development.

The recent report *Future options for regional agencies*, produced for Resource by John Holden (2001), has provided a very helpful analysis of the past, present and future situations and has laid down a route map to reach a single regional agency situation, allowing for the different levels of development across the country. However, Holden's recommendations are unequivocal in their support for the creation of one regional agency, flexible enough to accommodate regional variations, by April 2004 and sooner where practicable. Resource's role in enabling this process will be both practical, in terms of funding, planning and process, and inspirational in the creation of a clear regional identity and common sense of purpose and culture.

Conclusions

These are very early days. We have a long way to go in order to reach 2010. Nevertheless, the UK government has anticipated the impact of these developments by integrating its own oversight of museum, library and archive services through the creation of Resource.

Resource can encourage these developments and help bring them about through:

* strategic direction – overseeing the People's Network, drawing up standards for learning and stewardship, providing funding for integration at regional level
* advocacy – ensuring that the case for libraries and libraries funding is made in government; carrying out impact studies to demonstrate the value of library services; gathering statistics and conducting research to support its policy advice
* advice – showing the sector how it can increase its own resources by integrating its services to meet relevant policy agendas; explaining to government how the sector can contribute to lifelong learning, social inclusion, economic development and the quality of life; and helping citizens to appreciate how museums, library and archive services can enrich their lives.

In its *Manifesto* (2000), Resource's vision is that:

> Museums, archives and libraries belong at the very heart of people's lives, contributing to their enjoyment and inspiration, cultural values, learning potential, economic prosperity and social equity. (Resource, 2000, 2)

The *Manifesto* goes on to say:

> The task for Resource is to harness and develop these qualities in order to enrich everyone's lives, and to enhance the ways in which the sector is funded, managed, used and enjoyed . . . . To achieve this, our approach will identify and exploit the added value derived from partnerships. These will involve both links between museums, archives and libraries and links with other sectors, such as education, the media and the arts . . . . Co-operation through partnership will be the key to our success. (Resource, 2000, 3–4)

Resource is now living with the need to deliver that reality. We know that libraries have a central role to play in the knowledge-based economy, based on ideas, information and learning, and we know too that libraries are naturally inclined towards co-operation and collaboration. It is the responsibility of Resource, both officers and Board members, to remove the fear of loss of autonomy and identity, to cultivate an ability to enter into open and honest dialogue and to encourage a culture of trust and shared agendas. All of this will be necessary if we wish to engage with partners in order to reconfigure and transform library and information services for the new century and beyond.

References

Holden, J. (2001) *Future options for regional agencies*, London, Resource, available at
www.resource.gov.uk/information/policy/regagy.pdf

Library and Information Commission Education and Libraries Task Group (2000) *Empowering the learning community*, London, Library and Information Commission.

Nankivell, C., Foster, W. and Elkin, J. (2000) *People flows: investigation of cross-use and development of transferable strategies for co-operation between publicly-funded libraries,* British Library Research and Innovation Report 167, London, Library and Information Commission.

Resource (2000) *Manifesto*, London, Resource, available at
www.resource.gov.uk/information/policy/manifesto/mintro.asp

Resource (2001a) *Building on success: an action plan for public libraries*, London, Resource, available at
www.resource.gov.uk/information/policy/bosucc.pdf

Resource (2001b) *Library services for visually impaired people: a manual of best practice*, London, Resource, available at
www.nlbuk.org/bpm

Warren, G. and Dodd, C. (2000) *Futures together: accessing special collections in West Midlands libraries and related sectors*, Library and Information Commission Research Report 25, London, Library and Information Commission.

4
The regional perspective

Stuart Brewer

The landscape of co-operation at regional level among library and information services in the UK is complex, kaleidoscopic and confusing. At the same time it is shifting and changing rapidly, not only within individual library sectors and across those sectors, but also across the three domains that cover library and information services, museums and galleries, and archives and record offices.

The reasons for these rapid changes derive from the evolving perception of needs and opportunities at regional or local level and, in addition, from strategies driven primarily by central government. These strategies embrace a number of major policy issues such as social inclusion, regeneration, lifelong learning, modernization of government and devolution, as well as regional development, a dimension that the library and information domain has been slow to address even though a framework of regional co-operation has been in place since the 1930s.

This chapter outlines: the concept of a region and the background to recent changes in the concept; features that regions have in common, and some of the differences between them; examples of recent developments in co-operation within regions, with illustrations of how the library domain is coping with the need for co-operation; key issues, opportunities and constraints.

The concept of a region

The word 'region' can itself be confusing, carrying as it does a variety of different meanings. Within the European Union (EU), for example, the word is often used to denote a defined geographic area that has its own devolved government and a degree of autonomy below the level of a nation state; examples include Catalonia in Spain and Bavaria in Germany. In a wider context, the word is used more vaguely to refer to continents or large landmasses, such as the Middle East, the Americas, the Pacific rim. In the library world, a number of local library services may come together in a formal regional network: in the USA, for example, the Lewis and Clark

Regional Library System has 150 member libraries in 11 counties within the State of Illinois; and, in the Netherlands, plans are in hand for the public library of the city of Utrecht to merge with the neighbouring county library service into a single system for the whole 'region'. In the UK, major urban public libraries such as Birmingham, Edinburgh and Belfast have often been referred to as 'regional reference libraries' because of their substantial but informal role in meeting the information needs of large conurbations.

In the UK, the word 'region' is now generally used to denote the nine geographical areas in England defined as a result of recent central government legislation. These, together with the other three 'home' countries within the UK with devolved and elected government, namely Scotland, Wales and Northern Ireland, form the background for this chapter.

Traditionally, however, for librarians in the UK, the word 'regions' has meant the regional library systems (RLSs). These were established as voluntary, non-statutory bodies from 1931 onwards, primarily to facilitate interlending and other co-operative activity. They operated within agreed geographical boundaries (see Figure 4.1). The National Library of Wales and the National Library of Scotland were the service providers in those countries, and An Chomhairle Leabharlanna, the Irish Library Council, catered for Northern Ireland and the Republic of Ireland.

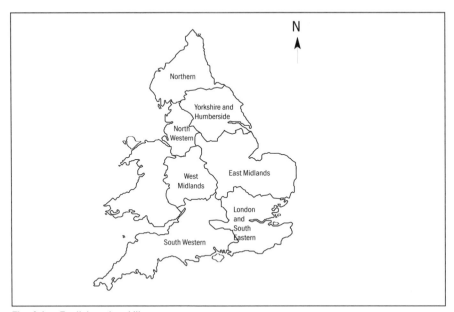

Fig. 4.1 *English regional library systems*

By the 1980s, the RLSs supplied a wide range of co-operative services to library and information organizations in the UK and Ireland. Members included nearly all public and university libraries and a number of other public and private sector organizations (CONARLS, 1998). The activities of the RLSs were more operational than strategic and were funded by subscriptions and income generation. From the 1980s, however, some RLSs were working with wider horizons and larger aspirations, seeking partners and funding opportunities for research, development and other strategic purposes.

This generally comfortable framework of regional co-operation was undermined in the 1990s, first by an increasing interest in regionalism on the part of central government, and second by legislation. As a result, the RLSs in England woke up to a situation where many other agencies in the external world were adjusting, voluntarily but pragmatically, to new regional boundaries as laid down centrally. One big issue was co-terminosity – should a regional agency adjust its boundaries to be in line with those now established by the government's framework for regional administration (Figure 4.2)?

In 1995, the then Department of National Heritage (DNH) commissioned a strategic overview of London's public libraries and their role in the social and

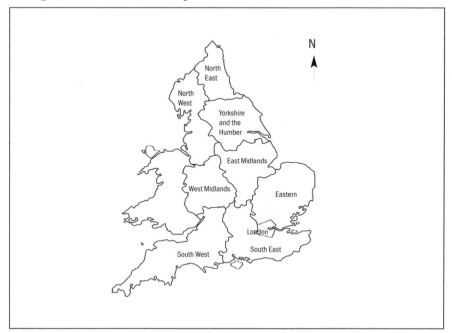

Fig. 4.2 *English Government regions*

economic infrastructure of the city. The consequent report recommended the establishment of a London Library Development Agency to promote the profile of the public library service, to lobby politically, and to establish partnerships and joint ventures with other London agencies (Burton, Greenhalgh and Worpole, 1996).

Expanding on this theme at a seminar on regional library development, Briony Lodge of the DNH's Strategy Unit, said 'The Department cannot achieve its aims by working purely at national level . . . . Each region has its own problems and opportunities in terms of economic development and regeneration' (*Regional library development*, 1996, 79). Duncan Wilson, Head of Libraries Division, DNH, added that 'Library and information services need a new, coherent regional strategy' (Which way for the regions, 1996). Wilson later cautioned the Library and Information Co-operation Council that 'library and information services could lose out unless they were capable of influencing and working with other regional bodies such as the Regional Government Offices' (Regional challenge, 1996).

With the election of the new Labour Government in May 1997, the pace quickened. Legislation was enacted for the devolution of government to an elected Parliament in Scotland, to elected Assemblies in Wales and Northern Ireland, and to an elected Assembly for one of the English regions, Greater London. Government proposals for the development of England's regions included the creation, in each region, of a regional development agency (RDA), which would promote sustainable economic development and social and physical regeneration and co-ordinate the work of regional and local partners. RDAs would also promote greater regional coherence and effective delivery of government programmes (DETR, 1997).

Not everyone in the library and information domain was quick to see the relevance of RDAs or their potential for enabling library services to enter more positively into the realm of regional policy, strategy and service development. In London, however, a further study concluded that a London Library Development Agency representing all types of libraries in London was both feasible and desirable (Interim Development Agency for London's libraries, 1998; Vision Research Consortium, 1998, 8).

Dramatic changes in government thinking, with a huge potential impact on library and other cultural sectors, were announced in July 1998 by DNH's successor body, the Department for Culture, Media and Sport (DCMS). These new proposals included better strategic and policy leadership, streamlined structures, greater co-ordination across the public and private sectors, and more devolution to regional level – the lack of a cohesive structure for delivering DCMS services at regional level was lamented. New cultural groupings were also proposed, and subsequently established as regional cultural consortia (RCCs), with boundaries congruent with those of the RDAs. Strong regional library bodies would be major players in the proposed regional structure, providing 'a regional focus of expertise and a *single coherent and efficient source of advice*' (emphasis added) (Devolution to regions, 1998; DCMS, 1998).

The phrase 'regional focus' closely echoed the main remit of the Library and Information Commission (LIC) set up by the DNH in 1995 'to provide a single, coherent and efficient source of advice to Government on all issues in the field of library and information services' and 'to draw the Government's attention to emerging issues and to suggest appropriate responses to them' (Memorandum of understanding, 1995). In effect, the opportunity was being offered to the English RLSs to develop a similar role and remit at regional level, though few of the RLSs were able to grasp the opportunity, partly because of a lack of resources, and partly because of a lack of vision and understanding of government objectives.

At the same time, however, clear-cut incentives from government for the RLSs to upgrade their aims and activities were notably absent. There was plenty of encouragement from the DNH and DCMS for RLSs to advance voluntarily in the way suggested, but no financial resources were offered to aid any such process. In the meantime, co-operative and collaborative initiatives and other joint ventures continued to emerge within and across the various library sectors, usually outside the traditional framework of regional library co-operation, and usually triggered or supported by new sources of funding.

A discussion paper from DCMS in 1999 further pressed the case for a stronger regional framework for libraries. It recommended that regional library bodies should represent a broad range of libraries, reflect Government Office geographical boundaries and work strategically and co-operatively with museums and archives within the region (DCMS, 1999).

A major issue, therefore, was not only whether the existing RLSs should reinvent themselves as strategic bodies, but whether they should adjust their geographical boundaries, where necessary, in order to be able to play an effective part alongside other agencies within their regions, or even whether completely new library and information regional development agencies should be established. The Circle of Officers of National and Regional Library Systems (CONARLS) commissioned research to clarify the key issues relating to co-terminosity and the role of regional library bodies in the new environment. This reviewed the changing strategic context at regional and national levels, and identified three potential models for regional library bodies:

- an integrated body for museums, libraries and archives at regional level
- separate bodies for museums, libraries and archives at regional level, which mix

strategy with service but co-ordinate priorities and combine for projects
* a separate regional library body as a service provider only, disengaged from regional and national strategic processes.

Other recommendations were that regional library bodies should be autonomous and should represent organizations across the whole of the library and information domain including: public library authorities, higher and further education libraries, schools, professional libraries, health bodies, workplace or special libraries and business information services (CONARLS, 2000).

Meanwhile, in April 2000, Resource: the Council for Museums, Archives and Libraries had been established by central government, replacing LIC and the Museums and Galleries Commission (MGC). Resource's *Manifesto* acknowledged the significance of the government's regional agenda in England, with the emergence of RCCs, the development of cultural strategies, and the activities of the RDAs. A fund of £600,000 was set up to stimulate cross-working between museums, archives and libraries: support would be given to help establish a pilot integrated regional body in the north east of England; and concordats would be developed setting out the way in which Resource would work with the devolved administrations in Scotland, Wales and Northern Ireland (Resource, 2001).

To summarize: until recent years, the word 'region' for the library world has denoted those ten areas of the UK covered by the long-established regional library systems. Now, however, the library world is in the midst of a lengthy process to adapt to the regional structure that has emerged from legislation set in train since 1997, that is the eight Regions of England, plus the Greater London Authority – all of these being co-terminous with the areas covered by the regional government offices and the regional development agencies – and the three nations, or home countries, of Scotland, Wales and Northern Ireland. In respect of regional library bodies, however, the library and information world in England is not yet synchronized with this new and hugely important framework of political reality.

Common features and differences between regions

In terms of the traditional library regions, the RLSs have a shared history and a core set of successful operational activities, which they co-ordinate within a national UK framework. They are voluntary, subscription-based organizations, whose memberships are mainly from the public library and university sectors, with a long-standing fruitful relationship with the British Library Document Supply Centre (BLDSC). They have tended to be inward looking, concentrating on the library and information domain, and generally slow to adapt to changing environments. None of them has in practice represented the whole of the regional library and information domain, and they have mostly had a low level of financial and human resources.

In fact, the similarities between the regions are fewer than the differences, regardless of whether the point of view covers the traditional library regions or the new government-driven regions. For a start, Scotland, Wales and Northern Ireland enjoy a considerable level of devolved administration from London together with, in the case of Scotland, a directly elected Parliament and, in the other two countries, directly elected Assemblies. In all three countries, this level of autonomy is giving politicians and public servants new opportunities and fresh incentives to investigate a wide range of social, economic, cultural and environmental issues, to collaborate with local authorities and other stakeholders, to devise and implement new policies, and to improve service provision for their communities. This should benefit library and information services. Scotland, Wales and Northern Ireland are coming to terms with being regions, with their own identities and cultures, within the EU. Increasingly, UK regions are exploiting the opportunities for EU funding.

The regions and countries of the UK vary considerably in size, shape, population, resources, wealth, geography, economy, communications, transport, politics, culture, history, identity and cohesion. Spending on public services per head in Scotland is 23% above the English average, 18% above in Wales, and 39% above in Northern Ireland. There are also major differences of this kind between the English Regions, although all are basically controlled and funded by government in London. However, this could change in the next few years: government is expected to produce a White Paper soon on the options for moving towards elected regional assemblies in England, enabling a level of devolution that could be comparable with that enjoyed by the other three countries.

Recent developments in co-operation within regions

The schemes outlined below are only a small selection from those existing up and down the UK. A larger number are described in a recent report on the co-operative concept (Education for Change and Acumen, 2000, Annex B).

Single sector

Organizations within a single sector, such as public libraries or higher education libraries, may find the prospect of co-operation particularly attractive. A shared framework of governance and funding, a common base of purpose and service provision, and a general feeling of everyone speaking the same professional 'language' should all encourage libraries to collaborate in order to achieve together what they cannot achieve individually or to do things better. Partnerships of this kind have generally focused on practical and operational matters such as resource sharing and arrangements for reciprocal access. More recently, however, libraries have seen the potential benefits in more strategic terms such as advocacy for their sector, influencing policy at higher levels, or being better positioned to interact with libraries in other sectors. In some cases an interest in emerging themes or techniques such as performance measurement or reader development may encourage libraries to work together, and the opportunities offered by information and communications technology (ICT), supported perhaps by new funding arrangements or by challenge schemes, have acted as a catalyst for libraries to form new partnerships. Again, partnerships that may have started out with merely practical or operational aims can, if successful, find themselves more strongly placed to move on to further projects or to a wider, more strategic level of activity, or both.

The M25 Consortium of higher education libraries links 125 college and university libraries that lie in the London catchment area. Formed in 1993 with the aim of fostering co-operation to improve services to users, its goals relate to access, resource discovery, collaboration and partnership – both cross-sectoral and cross-domain – and advocacy, marketing and communication. Its M25 Link Project, initially funded by the Consortium and the Joint Information Systems Committee (JISC), will provide users with simultaneous searching of member libraries' catalogues, while AIM25 (Archives in London and the M25 region) is a Research Support Libraries Programme (RSLP)-funded project to provide electronic access to collection level descriptions of the archives of over 50 higher education institutions and learned societies. The Consortium has strategic links with cross-sectoral and cross-domain organizations including the London Libraries Development Agency (LLDA).

The Consortium of Academic Libraries in Manchester (CALIM) was formed in 1992 by the libraries of the five higher education institutions in Greater Manchester to explore collaboration between university libraries. CALIM seeks to add value and increase access to resources through funding models, management structuring and legal agreement. It is connected to a broadband metropolitan area network. The possibility of Manchester City Libraries – the city's public library system – joining CALIM has recently been discussed.

Also within the North West Region of England, the Society of Chief Librarians

(SCL) has produced a regional strategy for its public libraries. SCL aims to work with other sectors and partners in creating a single, coherent regional voice for libraries and information services, to make the case for public libraries in the context of local, regional and national agendas, to develop joint working among public libraries and with other library sectors, collaborating with all the cultural domains. A prospectus has been published that illustrates ways in which the libraries' services link with the key issues of regeneration, ICT, social inclusion, lifelong learning, quality of life and partnerships (SCL (North West), 2000). The initiative is contemporary with moves by the North Western Regional Library System (NWRLS) to establish a new cross-sectoral regional libraries body, 'Libraries North West' (Capital Planning Information Ltd, 2000, 3–4).

The South East Libraries Performance Improvement Group (SELPIG) comprises seven neighbouring public library authorities that lie within the Greater London Region, linking up for information exchanges, benchmarking, training and reader development. Its original remit was the establishment of common performance indicators for use in the member libraries. This sub-regional group also acts as a consortium to seek external funding for new projects and, as a Stock Purchasing Consortium, it sought tenders in 2000 for a three-year contract for the supply of library materials (Olsen, 1998; SELPIG Purchasing Consortium, 2000).

Co-East, a consortium of six library authorities working to network 181 libraries in the East of England Region, began as a project funded by the DCMS/Wolfson Public Libraries Challenge Fund. Working with library system suppliers, content providers and an independent technical broker, the libraries are providing access to their catalogues and databases in libraries, in the workplace, at home, and in schools and community centres. The project brings their resources into a single virtual private network. Co-East has now expanded into a consortium of ten public library authorities, and has implemented the Co-East Plus Project, jointly funded by the British Library Co-operation and Partnership Programme and RSLP. A partnership of public, academic and health libraries, together with the British Library and the Open University, Co-East Plus aims to evaluate the technical, logistical and cultural issues involved in making resources available to users and create a regional internet gateway.

Cross-sectoral library and information services (LIS)

Increasing emphasis from government on co-operation, regionalism and value for money has helped to highlight the concept of development agencies: several such bodies have emerged within the library and information domain in England. Some are based on former RLSs, others are bodies newly created by library and information services within a region, but all have been set up in order to ensure that libraries become more visible and gain influence alongside the other key regional bodies that have been established by government, such as the RDAs and the RCCs. However, as with the RLSs and indeed with virtually all co-operative bodies in the library domain, these library development agencies depend for their basic income on the subscriptions of member organizations. No core funding is available from government sources and new projects have to be funded primarily from top-sliced funding sources or from other challenge funding schemes. Some of the other well-established cross-sectoral library bodies, which cover sub-regional areas within a region or even include parts of neighbouring regions, face the challenge of staying in touch with the demands of government's top-down agendas and with reshaping their own roles in a rapidly changing environment. Newer co-operatives, prompted perhaps by ICT developments and the availability of project funding, have opened up initiatives involving universities and major public libraries.

The East of England Library and Information Services Development Agency (ELISA) was established in 2000 as the single strategic voice for library and information services for the region, with representatives from public libraries, higher education, further education, health, workplace libraries and business services. Key priorities are the development of a regional library and information strategy that will support the strategic aims of the East of England Development Agency (EEDA) and of the RCC, and the brokering of strategic partnerships between library and information services and other agencies in the region. Anticipated outputs include promoting the value of library and information services and making input to decision-making about the spending of regional funds. A further objective is to develop relations with the museums and archives sectors at regional level.

The London Libraries Development Agency (LLDA) was set up in 2000 to develop a co-ordinated strategic vision for library and information services across London and to be the key agent for change and development across London's libraries. It works to forge partnerships and build links that improve the quality and scope of library services, to improve access and increase the resources available, to act as a first point of contact for those who seek to work with libraries and to make the case for libraries, using advocacy materials to stimulate debate about the role of libraries. LLDA will be a source of advice, information and expertise and promote examples of best practice. It has issued an ambitious library manifesto, which includes an aspiration to 'make London the leading Region for library innovation' (London Libraries Development Agency, 2000).

The Libraries Partnership – West Midlands (TLP–WM) was launched in 2000, replacing the West Midlands Regional Library System (WMRLS), which was founded in 1931. The new organization brings together the library and information services of the region's 14 local authorities and eight universities. Other libraries (such as college, health and workplace) will be brought in over time. TLP–WM provides strategic representation and advocacy, manages development projects and acts as a communications hub across libraries, museums and archives in the West Midlands Region, with links to West Midlands Arts and other key cultural agencies (see Figure 4.3). Current activities include the creation of a regional broadband public library network, development and delivery of electronic content and instigation of new bids and projects.

The RIDING Consortium includes all the university libraries in the Yorkshire and Humberside Region, together with the BLDSC and the City of Leeds Library and Information Service. RIDING was originally developed as part of the e-Lib (Electronic Libraries) Programme with funding from the JISC as a co-operative initiative to assist library users in the region by using internet technology to search multiple bibliographic resources. Other co-operative activities include access to secure databases, a searchable database of descriptions of regional library collections and online interlibrary loan.

SINTO: the Sheffield Information Organization is an information planning and co-operative agency of long standing. Established by the University of Sheffield, Sheffield Hallam University and Sheffield City Council, SINTO is a partnership of library and information services in South Yorkshire and North Derbyshire. Its aim is to improve the quality of information services through co-operation, planning and partnership by providing a framework for information organizations to work together; to develop co-operation as a means of achieving more efficient and effective services, thus contributing to the economic and social infrastructure of the Sheffield area; and to promote investment in information. In 1996, SINTO launched the Access to Libraries for Learning (ALL) Agreement for Sheffield, through which anyone who lives, works or studies in the city can use any of the public or academic libraries, both higher education and further education, for reference, study or research. In 2001 the scheme was expanded to cover the whole of South Yorkshire (a sub-region within the Yorkshire and Humberside Region), alongside a further reciprocal agreement with the public and academic libraries in Derbyshire (a neighbouring county in the East Midlands Region). SINTO is also exploring possible collaboration between libraries, archives and museums in Sheffield and is therefore unusual, if not unique, in operating as a cross-sectoral agency in both sub-regional and cross-regional modes, as well as having the potential to forge cross-domain collaboration.

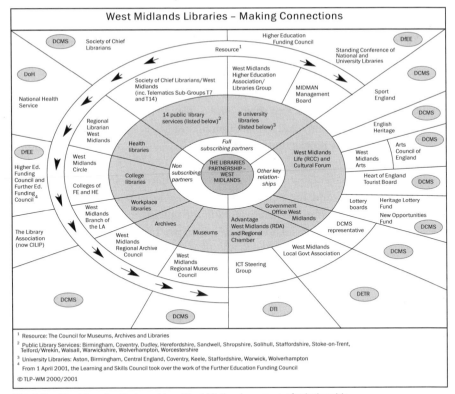

Fig. 4.3 *The Libraries Partnership – West Midlands: a map of relationship*

Hatrics: the Southern Information Network is the largest and most active information co-operative in the UK, working on the basis that the use of information resources is an important contribution to the economic well-being of its area in central southern England. Established in 1964, it is a network of 330 organizations based in Hampshire and adjoining areas who provide information services to each other. Among the sectors in membership are the libraries of government agencies and research establishments, hospitals, further and higher education establishments, companies large and small, and public libraries. Although the administrative centre of Hatrics and much of its membership lies in the new Region of South East England, other members are in the new South West Region. There is therefore considerable tension within Hatrics, with some members in the south west under pressure to look westwards, and some members in the south east encouraged to look eastwards, and Hatrics itself being as yet unsure of its potential attractiveness and relevance to the respective RDAs.

Regional/national

A few schemes involving regional co-operation are actually part of formal national schemes, supported by one or more of the UK's national libraries or by a professional body such as the SCL. From small, tentative beginnings such partnerships can experience a gradual build-up of achievement, confidence and credibility, to such an extent that they come to play a substantial niche role in the overall framework of library and information provision. As such, they can be viewed as one of the building blocks that could be used in the development of a national information policy.

NEWSPLAN, the co-operative programme for the microfilming and preservation of local newspapers and for making them accessible to users, involves public, academic and national libraries, archives, and the newspaper industry throughout the UK and Ireland. The British Library Newspaper Library plays a leading role and the National Libraries of Wales, Scotland and Ireland are major participants. A strength of NEWSPLAN has been its regional structure corresponding to the ten RLSs of the UK and Ireland, and it has long been regarded as a model of co-operation. It has embarked on the NEWSPLAN 2000 project, which is to preserve on archival microfilm 3500 UK local newspapers identified regionally as being in greatest danger of crumbling away.

Cross-domain

Collaboration across the library, museum and archive domains has been heavily influenced by the recent policies and actions of central government. The pressures to respond to these factors have been substantial and the speed of change required is a challenge for the professionals and organizations involved. While it is now expected that single regional agencies for libraries, museums and archives will be established in the English Regions from 2004, the future of existing regional library bodies remains unclear. In addition, although the main thrust of policy from government and from Resource is clear, the detail of implementation is being left to the relevant bodies in each region. Funding will be a key issue: it may be that member organizations and funding bodies will not be keen to support the current single-domain regional bodies as well as the emerging cross-domain bodies.

The North East Museums, Libraries and Archives Council (NEMLAC) was the first regional cross-domain body to be established following the creation of Resource in April 2000. NEMLAC, with three-year support funding from Resource, was founded in 2001 from two existing bodies: North East Museums (the Area Museum Council) and Information North (the Northern Regional Library System and development agency for library and information services in the north east). It is based on the belief that the three domains have a common purpose of information and inspiration, and that this outweighs what is distinctive about them. The objectives in NEMLAC's strategic plan are closely linked with Resource's manifesto and are grouped under the headings of advocacy, strategic development and best practice, with the aim of creating the conditions that will enable cross-domain developments to flourish. (Blackwell, 2001)

In the West Midlands Region, TLP–WM has developed a cross-domain think-tank in collaboration with the West Midlands Regional Museums Council and the newly created West Midlands Regional Archive Council. The outcome is a framework for libraries, museums and archives to work together in the region under the title Common Ambition and with the acronym WM.CLAM (the West Midlands Council for Libraries, Archives and Museums). This 'federal' approach will allow time for appropriate approaches to evolve and for other possible solutions, such as the cross-domain merger in the North East Region, to be observed and evaluated (Warren, 2001).

In the North West Region, the three regional bodies have signed a concordat committing them to work together for better co-ordination and strategic planning by, for example, organizing and encouraging co-operative work (such as ICT, training and conservation) and 'investigating the desirability and feasibility of a merger of the separate organisations to create a regional North West Museums, Libraries and Archives Council' (Concordat, 2000).

Yorkshire Libraries Strategy Group (YLSG) was established in 2000. The Group has a small initial representative membership, including representatives from the museum and archive domains in the region. As a result of the call from Resource for cross-domain bids, Yorkshire Libraries and Information with the Yorkshire Archives Council and Yorkshire Museums Council submitted proposals for cross-sectoral working that included the development of a strategic framework document for the libraries sector in Yorkshire.

Scotland, Wales and Northern Ireland

Developments in the non-English Regions of the UK, that is in Scotland, Wales and Northern Ireland, have demonstrated the importance to the library and information domain of having a direct relationship with government. As a result, progress made over the last decade has validated the 'development agency' concept for the domain, which has placed it in a strong position to benefit from devolution and to contribute to national policy-making in the respective countries.

The mission of the Scottish Library and Information Council (SLIC) is 'to provide leadership and act as the primary focus, co-ordinator and promoting agent for all library and information services in Scotland, and to support their work for the benefit of the nation and the development of its cultural life'. All 32 local authorities are members, as are all the Scottish universities, colleges and related art, cultural and information organizations. Funded by membership subscriptions and by the Scottish Assembly, SLIC's primary tasks include: providing leadership to library and information services and facilitating co-ordination; promoting understanding of the contribution of LIS; monitoring standards of LIS provision; and advising government on LIS matters. Recent publications include *Enabling seamless access: making the case for a National Information Strategy for Scotland* (1999). SLIC has regular meetings with the Scottish Minister responsible for library and information services (Miller, 1999, 6). The Director of SLIC was seconded in 2001 to advise the Minister for Enterprise and Lifelong Learning on the Digital Scotland programme. For an outline of library and information projects that contribute to Digital Scotland see Law and Nicholson (2001).

The Consortium of Welsh Library and Information Services (CWLIS) was established in 1997 to provide an operational forum for the information sector in Wales, to build on the Wales Library and Information Plan issued in 1993, and to function as an information development agency for Wales. CWLIS represents a wide range of information providers, including public, academic and special libraries, public organizations and the voluntary sector, fostering cross-sectoral co-operation. With 50 member organizations, CWLIS aims to facilitate the development of library and information services, to instigate research and innovation in library and information services, to influence policy and to lobby on behalf of library and information services.

Cydfenthyca Cymru – Interlending Wales (CC–IW), established in 1996, is the Regional Library System for Wales. In 2000 it received funding from the National Assembly for Wales to develop a strategic plan, consolidate existing services, identify a range of new services, form strategic partnerships with key participants in Wales and develop the participant base. This action plan was based on a report originally commissioned by the National Assembly in 1999 to examine the procedure for interlending in Wales. Among the key issues considered was 'the impact of "regional approaches" to policy-making and to the management of resources' (Roberts and Tyler, 2000).

The mission of the Library and Information Services Council (Northern Ireland) (LISC (NI)) is to maintain and enhance the standard of library and information services in Northern Ireland by providing advice to the Department of Culture, Arts and Leisure and other government departments, providing a representative voice for the library and information sector, and acting as a catalyst for development in library and information provision. The Council's action plan focuses on the role of libraries in lifelong learning, exploiting new technologies, the promotion of library and information services, and improving the provision of library services to children and young people. The Council is also surveying the apparent unevenness of library provision in further education colleges.

Key issues

From the documents and websites of the co-operative schemes outlined above, and of many other co-operative schemes, a number of key issues and lessons can be identified. The first is that government agendas and policies can be very powerful, especially when backed up by legislation and financial resources provided either direct from government or via government-funded agencies. The same will be true of any elected regional governments that may be set up in England.

It is, therefore, essential for the library and information domain to have effective development agencies or similar representative bodies in position to lobby government and to influence policy. In Scotland and Wales, for example, the prior existence of SLIC and CWLIS and their experience of working with the former Welsh and Scottish Offices have enabled them to be involved with the work of the new Parliament and Assembly. National library and information policies may well emerge in those countries, and perhaps in some of the English Regions, long before they do for England or for the UK as a whole.

All this helps to explain why new agencies such as ELISA and LLDA have been created, or why some existing RLSs such as NWRLS have been reinventing themselves as strategic rather than merely operational bodies. Agencies of this kind, whose geographical boundaries and spread of membership match precisely the new government regions, should enable the library and information domain to speak with one coherent voice and to be on an equal footing with the many other players and stakeholders at regional level. This would be welcomed by colleagues in other domains and by other regional agencies, who are confused by the large number of library and information services.

For these reasons, advocacy, visibility and the search for people to 'champion' the library and information domain are now widely accepted as essential elements for making progress, together with a much greater degree of evidence-based information about the value, impact and benefit of services to real users. Much of this can be more effectively pursued at regional than at national level, essential though that is too if national information policies are to evolve (Smith, 2001).

There have been many examples in the last decade or so of co-operative schemes that were initiated by the traditional RLSs, particularly the more dynamic, proactive and better resourced ones such as LASER, WMRLS and Information North. Increasingly, however, and largely because of the stream of generally unco-ordinated funding sources mentioned above, a wide and confusing range of schemes has emerged throughout the UK – single-sector, cross-sectoral, national, regional, sub-regional, cross-regional, single subject, and so on.

The RLSs, traditionally repositories of the co-operative impetus, have now been bypassed and overtaken. This is not to say that all co-operative activity in the library domain should be organized by or with the involvement of regional library bodies but, rather, that a stronger strategic framework might have been able to make better sense of the overall picture. Arguably, the emphasis on co-operation, with the necessarily fragmented and sometimes frenetic activity on these fronts, has impeded coherent regional and national development.

The future

There are major issues at regional level that library and information services need to address. Already in England there are the RDAs, whose government-set targets include promoting economic development, social cohesion and sustainable development through integrated local regeneration programmes. Libraries have much to contribute to these agendas, and much to gain by becoming involved with other stakeholders in helping to meet these targets.

There are signs in the other three countries that devolution can lead to closer working relationships between groups such as library regional organizations and the officials and ministers in their governments. Libraries need to capitalize on this, both in Scotland, Wales and Northern Ireland and in the English Regions. It remains to be seen exactly which of these regions achieve elected Assembly status and exactly how much administrative and financial autonomy will be devolved from central government. The opportunities for library and information services are already present, through RDAs, RCCs, regional government offices and the cross-domain working urged by the DCMS and Resource.

Issues of considerable relevance to library services will receive greater attention at regional level, including the quality of life in rural areas, the urban renaissance and the regeneration of city centres. Fresh thinking might well emerge on the role of metropolitan conurbations and the role of 'city regions'. In these contexts, the role and funding of the major regional libraries, such as Manchester and

Birmingham, as well as the potential for library and information planning at a local or sub-regional level, could be revisited. A Resource Task Group has recently reviewed regional museums and galleries, so why not regional libraries (Resource, 2001)?

The NEMLAC experiment will be watched with great interest. Given the strong regional identity and the keenness for regional government in the north east, there is a strong likelihood that it will be successful, in which case the pressure would grow for similar merged and joined-up bodies to be established in other regions and nations.

Resolving the issue of co-terminosity has also to be firmly pursued. Progress is being made with the recent creation of library development agencies in the London and East of England Regions, and with LASER's drastic, but realistic, decision to wind up its operations from the end of September 2001 (LASER, 2001). LASER spanned, either completely or partially, three of the new regions (London, South East and Eastern). Its departure clears the ground for the library and information domain to make positive steps in those regions towards a single, coherent library voice.

Regionalism is to be welcomed because it recognizes, and at best celebrates, diversity. A stronger regional identity should lead to clearer administration and to more streamlined links to regional government and other agencies. Enhanced regional identity will enable the library and information services to relate effectively to these bodies. The report *Mutual benefit* suggested that 'such cohesion engenders a real culture of co-operation in the planning and provision of all public services', although it added that 'it is difficult, if not impossible, to create social cohesion of this kind. Where it does not exist new building blocks for a co-operative culture need to be found' (Education for Change and Acumen, 2000, 23).

There are of course several constraints such as uncertainty and lack of confidence, lack of political awareness, and an inability to see the big picture or its relevance to library services. There is the continuous struggle to find adequate resources, both for core services and for the time-consuming work of creating and sustaining effective partnerships as well as the need for library managers to acquire the necessary skills for advocacy work and multi-agency collaboration. In addition, there are the difficulties of achieving joined up government – although regional developments could make this easier – and the confusing variety of funding and governing bodies for library and information services.

On the other hand, opportunities and incentives are in place to encourage the library and information domain to seize the day. There is already a strong political imperative to collaborate across sectors and domains, and this can be a legitimate and fruitful path to the achieving of service goals. The energy and performance of the new library development agencies, alongside that of already existing agencies such as SLIC, will be an example for others to follow. The experience of recent years suggests that more external funding opportunities will occur, whether for regional library bodies alone or in partnership with Area Museum Councils and Regional Archive Councils.

Waiting to see what happens, with the attendant danger of missing the boat, should be resisted. In spite of the challenges and difficulties, the development of library services at regional level is not one to be ignored.

References

Blackwell, I. (2001) New directions in North East England. In Brewer, S. (ed.), *United we stand: joint working between libraries, museums and archives. Proceedings of a seminar held at Stamford, Lincolnshire on 1 March 2001*, Loughborough, Capital Planning Information, 11–16.

Burton, C., Greenhalgh, L. and Worpole, K. (1996) *London: library city – the public library service in London: a strategic view*, Stroud, Comedia.

Capital Planning Information Ltd (2000) *Getting together: a regional strategy for the public libraries of the North West region*, Loughborough, Capital Planning Information, available at
www.nwrls.org.uk/together.htm

CONARLS (1998) *The library regions in profile*, 2nd edn, Manchester, CONARLS.

CONARLS (2000) *Carpe diem – seize the day: modelling futures for library regions in a changing cultural environment*, Newcastle upon Tyne, Information North. [For an account of the conference/seminar organized to discuss the *Carpe diem* report, see **www.thenortheast. com/conarls**.]

[Concordat] (2000) *Concordat between North West Archive Council, North West [Regional] Library System, North West Museums Service*, Manchester, North West Regional Library System, available at
www.nwmuseums.co.uk/html%20files/Concordat.htm

Department for Culture, Media and Sport (1998) *Comprehensive spending review: a new approach to investing in culture*, London, Department for Culture, Media and Sport.

Department for Culture, Media and Sport (1999) *Libraries and the regions: a discussion paper*, London, Department for Culture, Media and Sport.

Department of the Environment, Transport and the Regions (1997) *Building partnerships for prosperity: sustainable growth, competitiveness and employment in the*

English regions, Cm 3814, Norwich, Stationery Office.

Devolution to regions (1998) Report in *LINC News*, **27** (Summer), 1.

Education for Change and Acumen (2000) *Mutual benefit: a map of the co-operative landscape*, a study undertaken for the British Library Co-operation and Partnership Programme, BL Co-operation and Partnership Report 4, available at
www.bl.uk/concord/mapping/mappage.html

Enabling seamless access: making the case for a National Information Strategy for Scotland (1999), a consultative paper prepared by Ken Worpole, Comedia, [for the] Scottish Library and Information Council, available at
www.slainte.org.uk/slicpubs/enseamac.htm

Interim Development Agency for London's libraries (1998) Report in *LINC News*, **28** (Winter), 1.

LASER (2001) *LASER to plan its end on a high note*, Press release, 6 February.

Law, D. and Nicholson, D. (2001) Digital Scotland, the relevance of library research and the Glasgow Digital Library Project, *Program*, **35** (1), 1–14.

London Libraries Development Agency (2000) *London's library manifesto*, London, London Libraries Development Agency, available at
www.llda.org.uk/advocacy/manifest.html

[Memorandum of understanding] (1995) *Memorandum of understanding between the Secretary of State for the Department of National Heritage and the Library and Information Commission*, available at
www.lic.gov.uk/about/mou.html

Miller, A. (1999) National focus for libraries: leadership, *Metro* (newsletter of INTAMEL, the International Association of Metropolitan Libraries) (December), **17,** 6, available at
www.ifla.org/VII/rt3/news/metron17.pdf

Olsen, A. (1998) SELPIG: an emerging model of co-operation, *Public Library Journal*, **13** (2), 21–3.

Regional challenge (1996) Report in *LINC News*, **23** (Autumn), 1.

[Regional library development] (1996) *Regional library development – where next? Proceedings of the Regional Issues Seminar organised for the Department of National Heritage by the Library and Information Co-operation Council*, London, LINC.

Resource: the Council for Museums, Archives and Libraries (2000) *Manifesto*, London, Resource, available at
www.resource.gov.uk/information/policy/manifesto/mintro.asp

Resource: the Council for Museums, Archives and Libraries (2001) *Renaissance in the regions*, London, Resource, available at

www.resource.gov.uk/information/policy/rennais.pdf

Roberts, D. H. E. and Tyler, A. (2000) *Resource sharing by Welsh libraries: a report on interlending.* A report to the National Assembly of Wales, available at **www.wales.gov.uk/subiculture/content/libraries/lendcnts_e.htm**

SELPIG Purchasing Consortium (2000) advert in *The Bookseller*, 1 December.

Smith, P. (2001) Network traffic: where are the controllers? *The Library Association Record*, **103** (4), 228–9.

Society of Chief Librarians (North West) (2000) *North West libraries – making a difference: a prospectus from the public libraries of the North West*, Birkenhead, SCL (NW).

Vision Research Consortium (1998) *Feasibility study to establish a London Library Development Agency*, British Library Research and Innovation Centre Report 142, London, British Library Board.

Warren, G. (2001) The West Midlands: different solutions. In Brewer, S. (ed) *United we stand: joint working between libraries, museums and archives. Proceedings of a seminar held at Stamford, Lincolnshire on 1 March 2001*, Loughborough, Capital Planning Information, 17–22.

Which way for the regions? (1996) Report in *LINC News*, **22** (Spring), 1.

5

Co-operation in academia

Bernard Naylor

What's in it for me?

The legend of the ivory tower university dies hard. In the UK, in 2001 more than 30% of school and college leavers expected to go on to higher education, and this proportion was expected to grow to 50%. The higher education sector is the major contributor to 'blue sky research' output and is also an important player with regard to applied research as well. In respect of cultural amenities, some universities are substantial providers in their local communities, through their theatres, concert halls and art galleries. In all these respects, higher education commits itself to a community role, based on a careful, calculated assessment by each institution of where it needs to position itself in the world at large. Although idealism is by no means entirely to be discounted, there is a great deal of pragmatism in what higher education institutions do. Notwithstanding these factors, higher education institutions are still often regarded as 'ivory towers', isolated from the communities in which they are based. They are not automatically considered as institutions that interact strongly, through co-operation and collaboration, with the world outside or even with one another.

The same mixture of pragmatism and idealism characterizes the way higher education libraries interact with the wider world, whether it be the wider world of academe or beyond. Pragmatically speaking, libraries exist to serve their users, to meet their information and literature needs. For most, if not all, the time has long since passed when they could hope to satisfy, from their own resources, every need their users brought forward. Some measure of co-operation or collaboration with other libraries is one obvious way to make good the shortfall. An expectation of some degree of dependence on other libraries and sources of information carries with it the implication that the beneficiaries need to be prepared to be benefactors in their turn, if the circumstances call for it. At the most general level, this pragmatism can be expressed in two complementary questions: what additional resources does the library need? and, what additional resources can the library contribute? The resources of a library can usually be summarized under four headings: stock, technical infrastructure, accommodation and staff. This constitutes a useful broad framework in which to consider co-operation and collaboration and will provide the essential shape for this chapter. Although UK examples dominate this contribution, some foreign examples are cited, and many of the lessons may be regarded as universal.

Helping to meet the information and literature needs of library users is a fundamental feature of the profession of librarianship. Some degree of idealism is, therefore, often around when librarians are at work, and may even carry them beyond the limits that strict common sense might suggest. There is, also, no doubt that technical developments have greatly increased the possibilities for interaction among the members of any profession, for example through e-mail, bulletin boards, mailing lists and easier access to one another's publicly available information. As a result, the possibilities for co-operation and collaboration have been significantly enhanced, and this inevitably constitutes a temptation to librarians as well as an opportunity. There can be a 'feel good' factor about these types of activities, which takes the edge off salutary self-criticism. Idealism and pragmatism need to be complementary virtues, helpfully tempering one another.

Sharing . . .

Understanding the division of printed material between 'books' (or 'monographs') and 'journals' is a fundamental starting point. The degree of importance that they attach to journal content marks out a crucial difference between higher education libraries and public libraries. Differentiated already from public libraries by the greater extent of their journal holdings, higher education libraries are mainly looking for additional journal material when they call on resources elsewhere to satisfy their users' needs. The demands higher education libraries in the UK impose on the British Library Document Supply Centre (BLDSC, formerly the British Library Lending Division, BLLD) are overwhelmingly for journal articles, and the number of book requests they direct there or elsewhere is a small fraction by comparison.

The National Lending Library for Science and Technology

This demand from higher education libraries for journal content has strongly affected their approach to co-operation and collaboration, in so far as this is seen as a strategy for enhancing local resources. The watershed was marked by the founding of the National Lending Library for Science and Technology (NLLST), which began to deliver services from its renowned Boston Spa site in 1962. In the period before the founding of NLLST, higher education libraries had been major contributors to and users of the British Union Catalogue of Periodicals (BUCOP) and the World List of Scientific Periodicals (WLSP), the compilation of which represented a considerable co-operative and collaborative effort by all the libraries involved. NLLST was initially devoted to satisfying the demand for journal articles in science, technology and medicine, but it expanded its scope in 1967 to cover journals in the social sciences as well. By the time it was incorporated as an important functional unit of the newly founded British Library in 1973 (as part of the BLLD) it was regarded by higher education libraries as the one-stop shop for journal articles not held locally. In the 1970s, the usefulness of BUCOP withered in the face of the new BLLD service, and it was finally closed down in 1981.

The BLLD and the National Central Library

The emergence of BLLD changed the ethos as well as the service. Access to journal articles had previously been achieved by participation in the joint enterprise of BUCOP, with many libraries being contributors as well as beneficiaries. BLLD replaced this collaborative ethos with a publicly funded service, for which libraries paid a set charge as a part-contribution to costs. But this analysis should not be interpreted as a lament. BLLD flourished as a supplier of journal articles, and BUCOP declined, because the former was a more pragmatic option. The fact that the balance also shifted somewhat, away from the previous reliance on a more co-operative, collaborative, idealistic approach, was an accidental consequence.

Although the demand for 'books' not available in the local higher education library was a fraction of the demand for journal articles, some measure of demand did and does exist. While, in generic terms, it might be seen as similar to the principal interlibrary lending demand in the public library sector – also for books – it was different at a detailed level, with the required material being generally more scholarly and esoteric in nature. This could explain why higher education libraries traditionally involved themselves in a different interlending mechanism for books from that preferred by the public libraries. The latter showed a marked commitment to the union catalogues of the library bureaux, which had been established regionally before World War 2. The former placed more emphasis on supporting the national union catalogue of the National Central Library (NCL), even though some also supported their local regional bureau.

With the founding of the British Library, the NCL became part of BLLD. Higher education libraries continued to support the specialist union catalogues, for example, those relating to foreign language monographs, which BLLD maintained. They welcomed the further concentration of supply options caused by the BLLD's expansion of its own holdings of scholarly monograph material. And, by searching for locations in their own card catalogues, they also participated in the system of 'back-up libraries', which supported the BLLD's supply plan for the more esoteric items requested on interlibrary loan. Hence, towards the end of the 20th century, higher education libraries were familiar with a clear distinction between two supply systems: one for journal content in which they operated as the customers of a quasi-commercial service, the other for books or monographs in which they expected to supply as well as to demand, and therefore to participate in a co-operative exercise. However, both supply systems were managed by the BL, except for the smaller volume activity represented by the regional library bureaux.

The influence of the Follett Report

As the 20th century drew to a close, developments in information technology exercised an increasing influence on the document supply situation. Following an initiative from the University Grants Committee (UGC) in 1988, university libraries were offered financial help to enable them to make their catalogues accessible over the internet. Although the machine-readable data available did not tell the whole story, because the conversion of retrospective catalogue data to machine-readable form was far from complete, it increased the possibility that individual libraries, or their users, could themselves discover the location of wanted books or journal titles. In the aftermath of the report of the Joint Funding Councils' Libraries Review Group, which was published in 1993 and is usually called the Follett Report after Sir Brian Follett, the Chairman of the Committee (Follett Report, 1993), a programme of initiatives aimed at exploiting the potential of the information and communication technologies was set in train. This is usually referred to as the 'e-Lib (electronic libraries) programme' and included a number of experiments in interlibrary access and document supply. The most notable and enduring of these was London and Manchester Document Access (LAMDA), which initially involved higher education libraries in the two cities implied by the title, but later extended its scope. By the turn of the century, individual library users and higher education libraries themselves were showing more interest in asserting a greater measure of control over how requests for items not in the local stock could be satisfied. This clearly implied some measure of reversion to an approach based on collaboration and co-operation, rather than the one-stop client–server model implied by the British Library Document Supply Centre – as the BLLD had, by now, come to be called. However, it remained the case that most 'interlibrary' loan requests would still be forwarded to the BLDSC. The previous model had by no means been superseded.

SHARES

In addition, when the Research Libraries Group (RLG) in the USA began, in the late 1990s, to encourage their UK members, namely, the major UK higher education research libraries, which were also members of the Consortium of University Research Libraries (CURL), to use SHARES, their interlending system, they did not find the same enthusiasm for take-up that they had experienced among their US members. In effect, even the major UK higher education research libraries were mostly still saying that a system that did not take sufficient account of the paramount role of the BLDSC in the UK context would represent a degradation of the current level of service. The co-operation and collaboration model was still regarded as a fall-back, certainly for non-monograph material and possibly for book material too, rather than as the main supply method.

Co-operation with regional library bureaux and interlibrary access

So far, this account of interlending as a possible co-operative activity has concentrated on the needs of the higher education libraries and how their approach to supplying those needs developed and changed in the 20th century. However, it should also be noted that some higher education libraries have co-operated substantially with their own regional library bureau, especially in supplying information about their acquisitions and in meeting interlibrary loan requests, including requests from non-higher education libraries. For instance, out of all the libraries in membership of the system, the two libraries that, year on year, lend most items through the South-West Regional Library System are the university libraries of Bristol and Southampton. The explanation for this contribution to co-operation has to lie mainly in a degree of idealism or altruism, since neither library is a substantial borrower through that system, while both make considerable use of BLDSC. This example could probably be replicated with other higher education libraries, in other regions.

While interlending is a major and obvious approach towards the sharing of stock, interlibrary access – with or without borrowing privileges – is also a significant and complementary feature. The libraries of the older higher education institutions

71

have traditionally been cautious about allowing access to non-members of their parent institution. The main inspiration for this caution was the fear that, if restrictions on access were not imposed, libraries would be swamped by non-members. The likelihood of this clearly depends on a number of factors. How strong are the library's collections? How numerous is the local clientele that is likely to be interested in such collections? Does the library's location make it easy for non-members to make casual visits? A sensitive, case-by-case approach to these questions might cause different libraries to reach different conclusions about the likely level of non-member use, though it is by no means apparent that such an approach was always taken. Nevertheless, there is no doubt that the fear of being swamped has been a real factor, and has been accompanied by a feeling in some instances that, if the doors were once opened, it would be difficult to shut them again.

The 'library licence'

The historic basis for a more generous approach to access can be found in the so-called 'library licence'. The library licence, which formed part of the Net Book Agreement, was a concession from the UK Publishers' Association by which libraries could obtain a discount on the cost of new British books, provided that they allowed 'public access' to the material. The Net Book Agreement was effective in the UK for most of the 20th century, but lapsed when retail price maintenance on books ceased in the 1990s. Against the background of the library licence, a chequered picture on access has developed. Access to certain specialized materials, not readily available elsewhere, is permitted in some instances. The Standing Conference of National and University Libraries (SCONUL, now more correctly titled the Society of College, National and University Libraries) introduced a 'Vacation Reader's Ticket' scheme in 1965, by which students on vacation from one university were allowed reference only access to the library of a university near their home. Even within the federal University of London, access to the libraries of other University of London institutions by the members of any particular one has sometimes been a contentious matter, and borrower rights have not normally been conceded.

Old restrictions breaking down in the 1990s

Towards the end of the 20th century, however, there were increasing signs that the old restrictions were breaking down. Pressure for change arose partly through two action programmes, which followed the Follett Report, and a follow-up document completed in 1995 (though never actually published): the Report of the Group on a National/Regional Strategy for Library Provision for Researchers, called the Anderson Report, after the Chairman of the Group, Professor Michael Anderson (Anderson Report, 1996). The Non-formula Funding (NFF) programme, and the Research Support Libraries Programme (RSLP), which succeeded it, both channelled very substantial additional resources into higher education libraries to enable them to improve the accessibility of their strongest and most specialized collections, for example through improvements in cataloguing and conservation. However, it was made clear from the start that any award of funding was conditional on the collections being made accessible without charge to all members of the higher education community having a need to consult them. In practice, most libraries have taken this as a requirement to open up access to the whole of their holdings, rather than to distinguish between those materials that could be consulted by non-members and those that could not. This is an example of how funding from an external body can provide a stimulus, leading to improved collaboration among recipient libraries.

Three further examples can be cited to illustrate that the climate has changed with respect to interlibrary access. First, there is a small but growing number of interlibrary access schemes being developed within particular areas, usually a town or city, partly as a recognition of the general need to support the contemporary agenda of 'lifelong learning'. The cities of Sheffield, Southampton and Sunderland have all developed schemes of this kind, in each case including local higher education libraries, but attuned to what are reckoned to be the particular local circumstances. Second, there has been a further and important attempt to address the question in the large conurbation of London, embracing not just the institutions of the federal university, but other higher education institutions within the area ringed by the M25 London Orbital Motorway – hence the name, the M25 Access and Borrowing Scheme. The ambitions of the scheme range far beyond access, but access is an essential central component. Third, there is the UK Libraries Plus scheme. UK Libraries Plus was established in 1998, to allow reciprocal access and use of higher education libraries among members of the institutions adhering to the scheme, especially for the benefit of distance learning students, who were considered to have particular library access problems. The scheme was inspired principally by the more recently founded universities, especially the former polytechnics that had acquired formal university status in 1992. It is possible that they were inspired by their strong commitment to 'non-conventional' students of all kinds, including distance learning students. The scheme has expanded very quickly and now includes many of the older universities among its members.

If we see the question of access as a continuing struggle between the instinct to exclude, based on fears of intolerable levels of demand, and the instinct to admit, based on the professional inclination of librarians to make their resources available for use, the latter instinct is currently in the ascendant, and a symptom of the increased commitment to collaboration and co-operation currently observable among higher education libraries.

. . . and stocking

Supporting an interlibrary loan service, or underpinning an interlibrary access scheme are two obvious ways in which co-operation and collaboration can play a part in the immediate process of satisfying the needs of the user. However, there has also existed, alongside the immediate provision of services, the idea that, if libraries could only get together, they could share the task of acquiring literature in advance of demand, thus stretching their combined resources further and developing what would be recognized in the parlance of today as a 'distributed national collection'. Some public libraries took this idea furthest with the idea of a 'joint fiction reserve' in which the responsibility for long-term holding of UK fictional works was distributed alphabetically by author among participant libraries. Non-fiction publications recorded in the *British national bibliography* were similarly allotted for purchase to particular public libraries in accordance with their Dewey class numbers. Schemes of this kind were normally co-ordinated by the regional library bureaux to which reference has already been made.

Partial co-operative schemes

Higher education libraries too have taken some initiatives of this kind, but not with outstanding or continuing success. There has been no attempt among higher education libraries to divide 'the whole of the literature' as the public libraries did. In higher education libraries, foreign books, especially – but by no means exclusively – American books, have always been a major element in the total pattern of purchasing. Hence, unlike the situation in public libraries, there was no practical way of defining what 'the whole of the literature' meant. Instead, the emphasis has always been on partial schemes. Under the auspices of SCONUL, a scheme was drawn up in 1965 for sharing responsibility for acquiring copies of earlier British imprints, with individual libraries taking responsibility for a specific short period of publication, typically five or ten years. A similarly informal and unofficial scheme was inaugurated in 1966 by the Standing Conference on Library

Materials on Africa (SCOLMA), by which individual libraries undertook to concentrate on the acquisition of material from a particular country. The idea was that each library would then become known as the authoritative source for publications from the country on which it was concentrating. Both of these schemes were begun in a period when there was greater enthusiasm worldwide for co-operative purchase schemes of this kind, an enthusiasm that had already prompted the establishment of the Farmington Plan and the Latin American Co-operative Acquisitions Plan (LACAP) in the USA, or the Scandia Plan in Scandinavia.

Practical experience has tended to show that such schemes eventually wither away, as the commitment of individual member libraries declines, with or without any formal recognition of their demise. But traces of them do linger. Some individual libraries do continue to sustain their responsibilities long after other declared participants have withdrawn from their particular obligations, while some libraries that no longer actively participate may continue to exercise a curatorial responsibility for a collection of specialist material, which is otherwise dead and without significance. In an imperfect world, where nothing lasts for ever, a scheme that achieves something deserves credit for that, even if it also inspires regret that it could not be continued for longer.

Externally funded schemes

There ought to be more grounds for hope with schemes associated with a special injection of money. This not only overcomes the objection that there are no resources available to devote to a co-operative purchase scheme, but also introduces an element of accountability for outcomes to an external funding body, and enables the imposition of an obligation on the library in receipt of funds to make its acquisitions more widely available. In its day, the UGC, the body that used to have the formal responsibility for channelling government funding to the UK universities, funded a number of schemes of this kind in the field of 'area studies', especially for Latin American studies: 'Parry money' – in the 1960s (Parry Report, 1965), African studies – 'Hayter money' – in the 1960s (Hayter Report, 1961), Oriental studies – 'Parker money' – in the 1980s, and Slavonic studies (also 'Hayter money' in the 1960s). These special funds are usually called by the name of the principal originator of the report recommending their establishment. The University of London also established a Library Resources Co-ordinating Committee in 1973, which, for a time, used a system of subject sub-committees and earmarked purchase grants to encourage libraries to pursue the co-operative purchasing option. The Deutsche Forschungsgemeinschaft in Germany also offers a notable and long-lasting example of the use of earmarked funding to promote library specialization.

In favour of such schemes, it can be asserted that the overall inflow of material was usually enhanced; against, it can be said that any imperfections in the scheme became accentuated once special funding came to an end. Furthermore, such schemes may not make enough allowance for the typically shifting commitments of higher education institutions, the abandonment of former areas of academic concentration by some, and the emergence of others as major players in fields where they had been counted as being of no significance at the outset. The University of Essex and the then Portsmouth Polytechnic, now Portsmouth University, provided specific instances of the latter in the field of Latin American studies in the late 1960s and early 1970s.

Can libraries support the work of their academic staff adequately?

At the heart of these stumbling efforts lie two major questions, which relate closely to the proudly defended institutional autonomy of UK higher education institutions. Which institution will tell a newly appointed professor, with an outstanding research record and potential, that his or her research topic cannot be wholeheartedly supported by the institution's library because the topic has been allocated previously to another institution in accordance with a scheme of co-operative purchase? Which institution will affirm to a disappointed professor that the library's support for his or her subject has to be subordinated to the continuing support for a subject responsibility no longer given priority by the institution, but retained by the library as a residuary responsibility under a co-operative scheme? In an environment where the resources available are *verging* on superfluity – for, after all, which library ever admits to having *too many* resources? – this kind of long-term commitment may be defensible. Even UK higher education institutions with long memories may find it hard to identify a time when resources were so plentiful. In all of them, the idealism of contributing to a broader, greater good comes up hard against the pragmatic rock of the immediate demands of the existing academic community. As we shall see, each generation may address these perennial problems afresh.

Technological infrastructure

From the earliest days of the involvement of UK higher education libraries in library automation projects, the inherent potential of such projects to promote collaboration and co-operation has been recognized. But this potential has changed with the advance of the technology, and the position of the libraries has shifted correspondingly. The beginnings of the impact of technology can be readily tied down to the late 1960s and early 1970s. During this period, two important initiatives got under way, partly with financial help from the government's Office for Scientific and Technical Information (OSTI), which, in 1973, became part of the British Library as the Research and Development Department. The Birmingham Libraries Co-operative Mechanisation Project (BLCMP) was founded in 1969. As its name implies, it not only included the two major academic institutions in Birmingham, Aston University and the University of Birmingham, but also extended beyond the higher education sector into the public library sector. It placed particular emphasis on the sharing of catalogue records through the use of a common automated cataloguing system. The South West Academic Libraries Co-operative Automation Project (SWALCAP), also founded in 1969, focused more on the automation of processes and the sharing of hardware and software. Initial participants included the universities of Bath, Bristol and Exeter, the University College of South Wales and Monmouthshire (now Cardiff University), and the University of Wales Institute of Science and Technology.

As the technology evolved, the two projects expanded and developed their scope. In due course, they outgrew the initial stage of special additional funding and became financially self-sufficient. A predictable next step was their emergence as fully fledged commercial companies. By the end of the 1990s, BLCMP had developed a strategy based on individual processors in the member libraries, centrally provided software, and a centrally managed database of catalogue records. Members contributed records to this and had access to the database on a privileged basis, though the records were also made available on less favourable terms to non-members. SWALCAP had evolved similarly in respect of an increasing preference for local microprocessor-based systems, but, despite an initial low-key approach to the sharing of catalogue data, this had also acquired increasing importance for the members, and the data was also being offered to non-member libraries. However, having striven to develop its systems towards full exploitation of the most up-to-date technology, SWALCAP's successor company, SLS Library Services, was eventually taken over by an American company, Innovative Interfaces, in the 1990s and ceased separate existence.

These stories of the evolution of systems and services need to be placed alongside much larger, but parallel, initiatives in the US, especially the Research Libraries Group (RLG), with its Research Libraries Information Network (RLIN) system and the Online Computer Library Center (OCLC). In the US, the libraries in membership of these organizations integrated their services more fully with them. In particular, they saw the co-operative organizations as the main key to meeting their demand for interlibrary loans, not just as a shared computing and record-providing facility. Hence we can see, once again, the significance of the BLDSC service, which, in effect, deflected academic libraries from integrating more fully with a preferred library co-operative. But it must be emphasized that this represented an entirely rational and cost-effective policy choice in the circumstances.

The CURL database

It is appropriate here to refer to the CURL (Consortium of University Research Libraries) database, although further consideration of CURL as a co-operative will be found below. The CURL database of machine-readable catalogue records (COPAC) is an essential feature of the co-operative. Membership of the co-operative entails an obligation to contribute records to the centrally managed file, and entitles the member to draw records from the central file for addition to the local catalogue. The maintenance of the CURL database and the development of its content and facilities has benefited substantially in recent years from financial support provided by the Joint Information Systems Committee (JISC). JISC is a central body funded through the higher education funding system, and provides co-ordinating services and development funding for information systems. At the dawn of the new century, it is difficult to know what the future of the CURL database as a co-operative endeavour might be. If JISC support is withdrawn, the cost of maintaining the database may fall entirely on the CURL membership of about 20 libraries, and this may prove to be an exceptionally heavy burden. If JISC support, or some other form of central support, is continued, important questions will inevitably arise about participation in, access to and use of the database, and these may strike to the heart of the current basis of membership of CURL itself. In some respects, the options for the future of the CURL database summarize the dilemmas surrounding major co-operative initiatives in the UK. The environment is barely large enough to support a number of, probably, competing organizations. A comprehensive single organization, on the other hand, is likely to encounter difficulties over community of interest, since the libraries potentially involved differ so greatly. Then there is the role of money injected from outside. It can provide the stimulus to get libraries to work together, but what follows if the external funding is in due course wound up? The future of the CURL database may provide an answer to some of these questions.

Accommodation

For every library, space is a critical resource. The second half of the 20th century witnessed two major periods of heavy central investment in space for UK higher education libraries. The first followed the *Report on capital provision for university libraries* – called the Atkinson Report after the chairman of the investigative committee (Atkinson Report, 1976). The second followed the Follett Report (1993). During the first period, there were still two separate publicly funded higher education sectors in the UK: the university sector funded by the national government through the UGC, and the polytechnic sector funded through the local government system. It was the university sector that benefited from the investment. By the time of the second period, the government had united the two sectors, and was funding them through the Higher Education Funding Councils for England, Scotland and Wales and the Department of Education for Northern Ireland. The merging of the two sectors threw into even sharper relief the fact that many of the UK's larger cities contained two or three publicly funded higher education institutions and many more than that in the case of London. Although the possibility sometimes crops up in discussion, there has in fact been no significant attempt to encourage higher education libraries to share some accommodation, for example by pump-priming grants from the centre to fund low cost storage for materials attracting lower levels of use, or specialized storage suitable for rare and special collections. Nor has there been any instance of the sharing of accommodation between higher education libraries and public libraries.

The University of London Library Depository

The only significant example of accommodation sharing is provided by the University of London, which has developed a store for housing less used material on land provided by one of the constituent colleges of the University, Royal Holloway College, which is located about 20 miles from the centre of London, where land values are lower. The heyday of the University of London Library Depository coincided with the peak period in the influence exercised by the 'central offices' of the federal University. During that period, which lasted from the end of World War 2 until about 1980, three 'stages' of Depository, each housing about 250,000 volumes, were built as part of an overall plan, which envisaged eight stages and a capacity of two million volumes. The outstandingly 'co-operative' feature of this project lay in the opportunity offered to libraries to house some of their lower use material in 'co-operative storage'. In so doing, they relinquished control over the use of the material, even though their legal ownership was unaffected. In return, the intention was that 'co-operative storage' would always have the prior claim on the available space, over private storage, and items in 'co-operative storage' would not normally be duplicated. The first to deposit any particular item therefore got first claim on the space. However, in reality, the majority of the space in the Depository has always been used for private storage by individual libraries, as their own space problems have become more severe. Libraries normally used private storage with the hope of building additional library space on the institution's own site, and 'repatriating' the material sent to store.

Otherwise, by an interesting echo of the influence exercised by the BLDSC over the interlibrary loans system, libraries were encouraged to offer low-use material, which had come to be regarded as dispensable, to the British Library, as a way of ensuring that 'last copies' would not be accidentally lost. Hence, the UK higher education library community has never collectively shouldered ultimate responsibility for what is kept for the whole of academe, and under what conditions.

Staff and organizations

Throughout this chapter, there have been references to various specific activities of organizations, especially SCONUL and CURL. It is now necessary to set those specific examples into a broader scenario, which illustrates and analyses the role those organizations have played.

SCONUL

The most prominent and longstanding organization is SCONUL, especially since, in 1994, it merged with the Committee of Polytechnic Librarians (COPOL) to become truly representative of the whole higher education library sector and, even more recently, agreed to accept into membership higher education colleges that did not have full university status. Now 50 years old, SCONUL has always operated as a forum, an aid towards the definition of common policy positions, for example, on copyright, and an environment for mutual support, especially at the most senior level of library administration. With some exceptions, such as its important work in the field of management statistics and performance indicators, it has not been noted for running major programmes of activity, or for obtaining substantial grants from other bodies for the development of initiatives. Over half a century, the role of the central secretariat has also developed in a way that, it could be argued, matches what was happening elsewhere. There has been a shift in the balance, from an organization that depended principally on the outstanding operational library managers of the sector for the pursuit of its objectives, to one that looked more to a central secretariat funded by members' subscriptions, albeit with the members always retaining the ultimate control. This change has been accompanied by an increasingly professional approach at the centre, so that the organization has managed to match the growing professionalism and pragmatism exhibited by senior managers in the higher education sector itself. There is little doubt that the influence and effectiveness of SCONUL has increased correspondingly over the same period, and that its voice is now heard, in the highest councils of higher education and beyond, in a way that was much less likely 30 years ago. It is a matter for debate whether the change that has taken place represents a decline in the collective approach, which it might be argued was inspired in its earlier form by the true spirit of co-operation and collaboration, or whether we are simply seeing the same spirit discovering new ways of expressing itself in response to substantial change in the environment.

CURL

By comparison with SCONUL, CURL is a recent foundation. Established in 1984 to represent the interests of the major UK higher education research libraries, the 1990s saw it change from a mutual support organization, along the lines of SCONUL but with a smaller and more homogeneous membership, to one that additionally embarked on major projects envisaged as addressing the particular needs of its members. Although, from the beginning, CURL professed to stand alongside the co-operatives of the USA with major operational programmes, especially RLG, it functioned more as a specialist group along the lines of the Association of Research Libraries (ARL) in the USA until ambition and opportunity came together. The defining take-off point for this change of direction came with the foundation of the CURL database to which reference has already been made. But it is also noteworthy that CURL has become involved in other projects, not so ambitious in scope but also highly relevant to the future policies of its members, for example the Cedars Project (CURL Exemplars in Digital Archives) on the conservation of electronic publications and the union catalogue study, which was jointly funded by JISC, RSLP and the BL. As has already been mentioned, there are major questions about the future of the CURL database. They are closely linked with questions about the possible need for more union catalogues in the UK and, whichever way they are resolved, this is likely to have major implications for the future of CURL itself.

Local and regional groups

There is, in addition, a number of local or regional groups with modest programmes of collaboration, some of them having survived for a considerable period. They offer mutual support at a senior level, and some possibilities for joint training activities. Some have also defined conditions for interlibrary access and use among their members, especially for the benefit of users at postgraduate research level and beyond, but this latter type of development has largely been overtaken by UK Libraries Plus, which is now regarded as much more important. Perhaps the most ambitious of these schemes is the Consortium of Academic Libraries in Manchester (CALIM), founded in 1992, which benefits from the comparatively close proximity of the participant libraries and which has, as its clientele, a very large concentration of students in one major city. Even in this instance, the evidence is that the commitment to the consortium is a variable factor, affected partly by the outlooks of the senior librarians, academics, and academic administrators in the institutions concerned, and also, no doubt, by the presence (or absence), from time to time, of distractions from other forms of association.

A question of climate

Whatever the impression conveyed by the foregoing detail, it is important by way of conclusion to underline and account for the undoubted fact that there is a very positive climate in favour of collaboration and co-operation among UK higher education libraries as we press forward into the 21st century.

The Anderson Report, and the ensuing RSLP programme, to both of which reference has already been made, are undoubtedly highly important factors. The Anderson Report made clear its hope for the development of programmes of 'deep co-operation' among UK higher education libraries and, following the report, considerable resources have been made available, through RSLP, in support of specialized programmes that contain significant elements of co-operation and collaboration. Indeed, much of the post-Follett Report agenda, including, for example, a substantial number of e-Lib programme projects, has featured initiatives with a strong co-operative element.

Coming slightly behind, but equally symptomatic of the climate, the BL has emerged from its preoccupation with the difficulties of the major building project at St Pancras in London and has taken note of the populist approach of the post-1997 Labour Government towards the way our major national institutions operate. The practical result has included the BL Co-operation and Partnership Programme (BLCPP), which, albeit on a much smaller scale than RSLP, has funded collaborative projects within and across the various library sectors, and has drawn in a notable range of different libraries and different projects. Indeed, some projects have benefited both from RSLP and from BLCPP money, and there has been a conscious effort by the organizers to achieve synergy between the two programmes. At the end of the century, a BL/HE Task Force, in the words of the BL's Chief Executive, 'built a collective vision of an integrated national information infrastructure for students, scholars and researchers'. This has since been followed by the establishment of a Strategic Group for Research Libraries, chaired by Sir Brian Follett, whose 1993 report inspired the recent wave of higher education library development. This all fits well with the more general environment, encouraged by government, in which public sector bodies are being cajoled, by the offer of project funds, to work within the central government agenda, which itself emphasizes cross-sectoral collaboration as, for example, through the establishment of a single body, Resource, intended to promote collaborative programmes across the archive, library and museum domains.

Until the 1990s, it can fairly be said that those responsible for higher education, whether within the sector or in the councils of government, showed scant interest in library co-operation, except for addressing the occasional uncomprehending exhortation at the libraries themselves. The climate now is very different and there is strong interest, at government level and within the higher councils of academe, in promoting collaborative working. Furthermore, JISC is a powerful body with a substantial budget and staff, significant authority and an emerging core of policy, such as the distributed national collection (DNC) and the Distributed National Electronic Resource (DNER). It is very much in the interest of individual libraries to collaborate with the JISC agenda – which is not at all meant to imply that the agenda is suspect.

What has to be recognized, however, is the historic fact that co-operation and collaboration among libraries are not new. The shine that characterizes them at present is the shine of refurbishment. Periodic injections of additional funding have always been one of the keys as to whether, at any given time, things have been going well for library co-operation or badly. Given the current level of outside interest and the recent injection of substantial additional resources, it is not surprising that co-operation is a high-profile current theme. What has to be uncertain is whether this will survive long-term or whether it will turn out to be another temporary surge, which will, in due course, expend itself. However, even if the surge turns out once more to be temporary, it will probably be possible to look back and see that it has delivered significant benefits, some of which will be as near permanent as anything in this impermanent world.

References

[Anderson Report] (1996) Joint Funding Councils' Libraries Review, *Report of the Group on a National/Regional Strategy for Library Provision for Researchers*, available at
www.ukoln.ac.uk/services/elib/papers/other/anderson/

[Atkinson Report] (1976) University Grants Committee, *Report on capital provision for university libraries*, London, HMSO.

[Follett Report] (1993) Joint Funding Councils' Libraries Review, *Joint Funding Councils' Libraries Review Group: report*, available at
www.ukoln.ac.uk/services/papers/follett/report/

[Hayter Report] (1961) University Grants Committee, *Report of the Sub-committee on Oriental, Slavonic, East European and African Studies*, London, HMSO.

[Parry Report] (1965) University Grants Committee, *Report of the Committee on Latin American Studies*, London, HMSO.

6

Co-operation in preservation

Stephanie Kenna and Helen Shenton

Introduction

When collaborative preservation works well it makes things happen and raises individual, institutional and professional profiles. Successful co-operation is driven by both timeliness and by institutional and professional will: when a balance is achieved between altruism and institutional self-interest to create something of value to the individual institution and something of greater value than the sum of the contributions of individual institutions. Nevertheless, behind every successful collaboration, there are usually one or more individuals on whose enthusiasm and determination the whole enterprise depends. Successful collaboration in the field of preservation also makes the precarious transition from theory to practice. The most risky time is during the translation from theory and 'talking' to the practicalities of 'doing'. Much worthy preservation research and many collaborative preservation ideas never reach fruition, partly because of poor timing and partly because of lack of individual and institutional enthusiasm and willpower.

Co-operation is generally deemed to be a 'good thing' and the current political and economic climate in the UK favours co-operative preservation. Government agendas encourage the development of regional and national initiatives building on regional and national culture and identity; there is a growing recognition that no one institution can have encyclopaedic holdings, while advances in information communication technology make the concept of distributed national resources, their management and preservation, a reality. Level or reduced funding, both for the preservation of materials in traditional formats and for the new and fast moving digital environment, are driving libraries, museums and archives to consider working collaboratively. Political initiatives emphasize the need for connected thinking across sectors and across domains. Co-operative initiatives are more likely to materialize if the same need or solution is identified by a number of different bodies.

Collaboration costs. While often undertaken with the aim of resource sharing, it has its own direct, and indirect costs. Collaborative preservation is less likely to be successful if weighed down by administration or where initiative-overload prevents proper engagement by key individuals. Lack of progress can also occur when so many organizations or groups see something needs to be done, that no one actually does anything. When co-operation does not work well it can stifle individual initiative. If the aims are too diverse it may stall because of the size of the remit and the interdependence of too many elements.

Preservation here is defined as covering 'all managerial and financial considerations including storage and accommodation provision, staffing levels, policies, techniques and methods involved in preserving library and archive materials, and the information contained therein' (Foot, 2001, 1). We would also include digital preservation and research into preservation management and conservation techniques.

Working together to ensure the preservation of the documentary and cultural heritage in analogue and digital formats for long-term access is a key strand of preservation strategy at all levels: local, regional, national and international. Preservation management issues are of global relevance. They are not constrained by domain specific concerns. Preservation solutions are often expensive and everyone has limited resources. Conversely, new techniques are widely transferable. Digital preservation is a rapidly changing area where emerging solutions and standards are globally applicable. This chapter is intended to present a snapshot of some of the current and recent significant collaborative preservation initiatives in libraries and archives in the UK and internationally at September 2001, with comment on the features and characteristics that contributed to success.

Such a snapshot of collaborative preservation initiatives has not been made in this way before (for example, see Eden and Gadd, 1999). This overview will be divided into those initiatives that are primarily project-based, organizational mechanisms, and those that are strategic, although different strands of more complex initiatives may fall into more than one category.

Projects

A project entails 'doing': working together to achieve specific results usually, though not always, within a specific timescale. Projects are usually successful where there are practical conclusions; they are less likely to be successful where theory and good ideas do not translate into practice.

Project-based initiatives are often dependent on external sources of funding. The main problems are the lack of central co-ordination and phasing of funding opportunities, and the need to maintain sustainability and momentum beyond the period of funding. In addition, the purpose for which funding is available may not necessarily match need and one institution has to be prepared to act as the lead partner and take responsibility for completion.

Responding to funding opportunities

A feature of recent years (not only in the UK) has been the gradual development of a competitive bidding culture for the allocation of scarce public resources, together with a requirement by the various funding bodies to work in partnership. The first Call for Proposals to the British Library Co-operation and Partnership Programme (BLCPP) in 1999 welcomed collaborative and partnership approaches to the retention and preservation of resources to ensure long-term access. Funded projects included a mass deacidification study and the implementation of a digital materials workbook in libraries.

A feasibility study was undertaken by a consortium of national and university libraries, local record offices and the National Preservation Office (NPO) and led by the National Library of Wales to investigate and make recommendations for a collaborative approach to mass deacidification as part of the national preservation strategy for the cultural written heritage. Follow-up work is now in hand to draw up a draft tender specification for a mass deacidification facility and for a pilot group of institutions in London and south east England to carry out surveys of their collections and determine the level of acid deterioration (Rhys-Lewis, 2001). The project is moving towards the crucial stage where theory must translate into practice and the collaborative approach could provide a powerful voice for funding for the implementation phase. The involvement of prominent institutions in both the feasibility and pilot studies should, however, be a significant factor in promoting the concept more widely. A collaborative approach between national archives and national library has succeeded in other countries, for example the Netherlands and Canada. This probably represents the last and best chance for the development of bulk deacidification facilities in the UK. It was a feature of the Library of Congress-led US deacidification development programme that it took several attempts before a commercially viable solution was established.

The Arts and Humanities Data Service (AHDS) at King's College London worked with the British Library (BL), the NPO and two other partner institutions to test the research from a previous study on the preservation management of digital materials and to explore its potential to support collaboration in digital archiving. The resulting *Digital materials workbook* was compiled and tested by people with experience in the field. The intention is that it will be kept up to date by the UK Digital Preservation Coalition (DPC; see below) to reflect new developments in the field. This project has made a successful transition from the initial research to a very practical result (Jones, M., 2001; Beagrie and Jones, 2001a; Beagrie and Jones, 2001b).

An opportunity to bid for funding for the Survey on Conservation of Asian Documents (SCAD) project, led by the Bodleian Library in Oxford, was presented by the collaborative collection management strand of the Research Support Libraries Programme (RSLP) for the UK higher education sector. The survey will assess the current physical condition and storage environments of UK Asian document collections, as a first step towards formulating preservation, conservation and access strategies for the collections. Surprisingly, out of 17 projects funded in this strand, this was the only one with a preservation component.

RSLP also provided funding for three conservation units at Dundee, Southampton and Leeds University Libraries in order to provide a high-quality regional facility for the higher education sector. RSLP funding enabled the units to provide a subsidized conservation service on a reducing scale over a three-year period. A variety of services are offered but, as the subsidy falls and prices rise, sustainability beyond the period of funding may prove to be a problem, unless the units can successfully diversify into other sectors. The need to develop an assured market may well have inhibited the development of shared conservation facilities in other sectors and regions, though conservation units often offer services outside their parent institution to raise additional revenue. Paradoxically, practical conservation projects themselves often depend on the availability of external funding. Another type of approach, which brings together several local conservation agencies, including museums and the University of Southampton Library, is the Southern Conservation Network (SCN) launched in 2000 with a grant from the former Museums and Galleries Commission (MGC). The Network is based on sharing expertise and resources rather than facilities and also aims to promote professional practice and foster collaborative research. This looser approach may prove to be more viable.

Doing things together

A funding opportunity may enable institutions to undertake projects at regional, national or international level, which they could not do alone. Examples include the Mellon Microfilming Project and NEWSPLAN in the UK, digital archiving projects funded by the Andrew W. Mellon Foundation in the USA and the internationally collaborative work of the joint Online Computer Library Center (OCLC)/Research Libraries Group (RLG) Working Group on Metadata for Digital Preservation.

The Mellon Microfilming Project was a major national co-operative programme of preservation microfilming in the UK, funded by the Andrew W. Mellon Foundation of New York from 1988 to 1997. The programme was managed collaboratively by a steering committee, chaired by the NPO and including representatives of the BL, the National Libraries of Wales and Scotland, Cambridge University Library, the Bodleian Library and Trinity College Dublin. A programme of microfilming, which included manuscript collections, trade journals and monographs, and 19th century fiction, was carried out in the partner institutions, while grants totalling over £1 million were awarded for preservation microfilming in 13 other UK institutions – categories of material here included monographs, periodicals, tracts and pamphlets, and directories. Over 12,500 reels of high quality preservation microfilm were produced, the profile of preservation microfilming was raised and standards for preparation and filming practices were developed and promoted. Preservation microfilming is now an accepted preservation medium in the UK and the manual of the Mellon Microfilming Project, recently revised by the NPO as the *Guide to Preservation Microfilming*, is the recognized standard (National Preservation Office, n.d.; National Preservation Office, 2000). It is unlikely that progress on this scale would have been possible without a collaborative national approach or large-scale external project funding.

NEWSPLAN, a national programme for the microfilming and preservation of local newspapers and making them accessible to users, began in 1986. It involves public libraries, record offices, national libraries and the newspaper industry. Initially led by the BL, with local input in kind and a contribution to filming, NEWSPLAN has now achieved a local and regional momentum, which resulted in a successful bid in 1999 to the Heritage Lottery Fund (HLF), the major source of funding in the UK for heritage conservation (Matheson, 1998). In this case the collaborative approach enabled the development of a more powerful voice for fundraising than could have been achieved by institutions and organizations acting alone.

Building on its earlier work on preservation microfilming, the Andrew W. Mellon Foundation is now working in the USA with the Digital Library Federation (DLF), the Council on Library and Information Resources (CLIR) and the Coalition for Networked Information (CNI) in the area of digital preservation. In early 2000, the DLF, CLIR and CNI brought together librarians, publishers and licensing specialists to address issues surrounding the archiving of electronic journals. A consensus on the minimum requirements for e-journal archives was reached and the Foundation solicited proposals from a number of US research libraries to help plan the development of e-journal repositories meeting those requirements. Seven libraries were awarded grants in February 2001, namely the New York Public Library and the university libraries of Cornell, Harvard, MIT, Pennsylvania, Stanford and Yale. Yale, Harvard and Pennsylvania are working with individual publishers on archiving the range of their electronic journals. Cornell and the New York Public Library will work on archiving journals in specific disciplines. MIT's project involves archiving 'dynamic' e-journals that change frequently, and Stanford's involves the development of specific archiving software tools (full details of the projects are available at **www.diglib.org/preserve/ejp.htm**).

Metadata, or data about data, is at the heart of preserving and making accessible digital information. The joint OCLC/RLG Working Group on Metadata for Digital Preservation aims to identify and support best practices for the long-term preservation and retention of digital objects. A consensus-building approach was used here to identify a comprehensive metadata framework, which would support a broad range of digital preservation activities. A White Paper, published in January 2001, describes current thinking and practice. Beginning with a definition of preservation metadata, it progresses to a discussion of high-level requirements for a broadly applicable framework, highlights the Open Archival Information System (OAIS) reference model as a common starting point, and reviews existing metadata element sets from projects and institutions that were informed by the OAIS model during their work. These include the Consortium of University Research Libraries (CURL) Exemplars for Digital Archives (Cedars) project in the UK, the Networked European Deposit Library (NEDLIB) led by the Koninklijke Bibliotheek (KB) in the Netherlands and work carried out at the National Library of Australia. The comparison identified areas of convergence and divergence between these applications. The Working Group now aims to develop a comprehensive metadata framework, identify the essential preservation metadata elements required to support it, identify and evaluate alternative implementation approaches and make recommendations for best practices or approaches in implementing preservation metadata (OCLC/RLG Working Group on Preservation Metadata, 2001).

Sharing resources

Collaboration enables institutions to share and make better and more effective use of limited resources, though the corollary is that working together can be expensive with both hidden and opportunity costs. Such initiatives have a specific result and funding may be sought for the initial investment, but they aim ultimately to be self-supporting.

This approach to sharing resources is particularly suited to disaster preparedness. An example at regional level is provided by the Disaster Management Group of the M25 Consortium of Higher Education Libraries, a membership organization of higher education libraries within the area ringed by the M25 London Orbital Motorway. The aim of the Group is to promote awareness and best practice in disaster control management, including disasters affecting IT-based services; to assist in the dissemination of information on disaster control management; to undertake co-operative initiatives such as investigating joint purchasing opportunities. The Group provides a framework for planning, facilitates a rapid response and sharing of skills and provides business continuity. A planning and advisory tool for disaster preparedness is available on the Consortium's website. The Consortium Action and Business Plan for 2000–3 allows pump priming funding of £1000 per annum for the first two years from members' subscriptions for the purchase of training and supplies, after which member institutions are expected to be self-supporting.

The Regional Emergency Disaster Squad (REDS), established in 1991 and co-ordinated by the East Midlands Museums Service, is another type of regional approach, which brings together museums, libraries and archives. REDS offers members a 24-hour call out service and has access to stockpiles of emergency salvage materials. It also offers training days and has produced an emergency manual, which contains information on risk reduction and advice on disaster containment, and recommends that stockpiles of salvage material be kept.

At the international level is the Blue Shield initiative, the cultural equivalent of the Red Cross. The Blue Shield is the symbol specified in the 1954 Hague Convention for marking cultural sites to give them protection from attack in the event of armed conflict and the International Committee of the Blue Shield (ICBS) exists to work to protect the world's cultural heritage threatened by wars and natural disasters. The United Kingdom and Ireland Blue Shield Organisation covering libraries, archives and museums was launched in March 2001 by the NPO to support the international initiative and to raise national awareness of the threats to the cultural heritage. A Netherlands Blue Shield was set up in June 2000 and initiatives are also underway in Canada, France and Belgium. There is a risk that Blue Shield could be over-ambitious and resource intensive. The UK initiative has set a realistic and achievable five-year programme of work, which includes the development of a funding strategy.

Cross-domain fertilization

Projects provide a mechanism whereby a wide range of institutions, experience and expertise can be brought together to seek solutions to identified problems. These include museums, galleries, archives and libraries; cultural and academic institutions; or curators, conservators and scientists. Such cross-fertilization between different sectors and disciplines provides an environment for creativity and innovation as well as practical results.

Although there are differences between the museums, galleries, libraries and archives domains, there are also areas of convergence and overlap, particularly within the field of collections care. A good example is the development of a methodology for preservation needs assessment. The Preservation Administrators Panel (PAP) of the NPO identified the need for a survey tool that would help libraries assess their preservation requirements and facilitate the assessment of national preservation needs and priorities, thereby contributing to the development of a UK national preservation policy. This coincided with the establishment in 1997, by the former British Library Research and Innovation Centre (BLRIC), of a research programme for the preservation of, and access to, the recorded heritage, together with the opportunity to bid for funding for a cross-disciplinery research team of librarians, conservators and statisticians to develop a survey method. Drawing on survey methodology used in libraries in the USA and UK, in museums and in archives, the team developed a method for assessing the preservation need of any library collection by examining 400 items with 95% confidence (Eden et al. 1998; Dungworth and Wakeling, 1999). This was subsequently piloted and refined by the NPO in partnership with the institutions represented on PAP, developed and validated by the BL and extended to archives in collaboration with the Public Record Office (PRO) (Jones, S., 2000). The NPO Preservation Assessment Survey is now being introduced to libraries and archives in the UK to create a picture of national preservation needs and is also being developed for use in museums. The adoption and validation of the survey by a number of prominent institutions, including the BL, together with its promotion by the NPO, was a significant factor in ensuring that the original research was translated into a practical programme of work and accepted by the wider community.

The concept of levels of collections care, originating in the UK museum community, is another area where research in one domain has proved transferable (Museums and Galleries Commission, 1998). Research funded by the former Library and Information Commission extended the concept to libraries. Ten key areas of library activity that have an impact on the long-term preservation of collections, such as environmental monitoring and control, storage, and handling materials, were agreed and used as the framework for a benchmark system. This identifies levels of performance in the categories 'basic', 'good' and 'best' in order to help libraries evaluate how well they are caring for their collections and identify areas where improvement might be needed (Bell and Lindsay, 2000). This, too, was subsequently extended to archive collections with funding from Resource: the Council for Museums, Archives and Libraries and has been further refined for museums. *Unified benchmarks for collections care* covering museums, libraries and archives was published by Resource early in 2002.

Photographs form a category of material particularly well suited to collaborative activity. Not only are they to be found in many different types of institution and collections, including commercial picture libraries, but, as a genre, they also particularly lend themselves to digital technology, and have very specific preservation requirements. In 1999, the European Commission on Preservation and Access (ECPA), with European Union (EU) funding under the Culture 2000 programme, initiated a project to investigate the long-term preservation of all kinds of photographic materials and define the role of new technology in collection management. The Safeguarding European Photographic Images for Access (SEPIA) project brought together a variety of institutions holding collections of photographs and encompassed a survey of conservation and digitization of photographic collections, expert meetings and workshops, guidelines on best practice and use of standards, an open conference and a website. A three year follow-up programme has been funded in the latest Call for Proposals of Culture 2000 (Browne, 2000). High administrative overheads militated against any one institution taking the lead, which is a characteristic of such funding, and the ECPA took on that overhead for all.

Fusing the arts and the sciences

There has been no detailed analysis of the gaps in library preservation and conservation research specifically in the UK, though a recent report, commissioned by the CLIR and distributed in Europe by the ECPA, provides a useful, up to date map of current research activities worldwide and identifies a number of broad areas that urgently need attention (Porck and Teygeler, 2001). However, an exercise undertaken by the American Institute for Conservation (AIC) had an interesting finding, which was that the need was not so much for research and its publication, but for the dissemination and absorption of existing research results (Hansen and Reedy, 1994). This is equally true of the UK scene. No library or archive in the UK has dedicated scientific facilities or personnel, nor are there centralized research facilities, such as the Centre de Recherches sur la Conservation des Documents Graphiques (CRCDG) in France or the Canadian Conservation Institute (CCI). Collaboration between academic research departments and cultural institutions has, however, enabled the application of technical equipment and expertise to the study, analysis and understanding of historical materials and collections. The notion of conservation as a fusion of the arts and the sciences may have been over-stated, but it is probably this element that is responsible for successful partnership in this area.

Examination and analytical techniques are particularly conducive to collaboration. Use of Ramen laser spectroscopy at University College London to identify pigments and inks in medieval manuscripts at the BL, and in Indian Mughal albums at the Victoria and Albert Museum, represents the drawing together of several strands: a cultural and an academic institution; scientists, curators and conservators; history, art and science. The University research department not only has advanced analytical equipment and the skilled technical staff to use it, but also students and researchers seeking innovative research projects (Jacobs and Brown, 2001). Similarly, the application of National Aeronautics and Space Administration (NASA)-developed imaging technology by the University of Kentucky to the fire-damaged Beowulf manuscript at the BL to reveal text concealed by previous restoration or obscured by burn damage and erasures, or the use of digital manipulation by the University of Washington to re-create and read fragments of early Buddhist manuscripts at the BL, have been successful because the academic institutions have the methods and the technology for addressing questions posed by the collections.

The application of the study of microenvironments to the development of showcase design for exhibition galleries is another example of the successful application of science in the cultural sector. Moreover, the environmental conditions of collections, from the burgeoning uses of anoxic (oxygen-free) environments for storage (and even display, and salvage) to the preservation index datalogger, are a particularly fruitful area of collaboration.

The International Dunhuang Project (IDP) illustrates co-operation between different countries with different conservation and preservation cultures. The IDP is part of the Electronic Cultural Atlas Initiative (ECAI) led from the University of California, Berkeley. Its aim is to bring together, electronically, all the manuscripts and printed documents from Chinese Central Asia dating from the fifth to the tenth centuries, in particular the 40,000 Buddhist manuscripts found in Cave 17 in Dunhuang, Gansu Province, China. These are now housed in four major institutions: the National Library of China, the BL, the Bibliothèque Nationale de

France, and the Institute of Oriental Studies, St Petersburg, with smaller holdings elsewhere. None of those institutions can offer full access to its collections for various reasons: the poor condition of the manuscripts, the lack of a complete finding list or the policy of the institution. The project also aims to develop new techniques for the preservation of the original documents through close collaboration with research chemists and paper technologists; to promote common standards of preservation methods and documentation; to store the documents in the best possible environment and reduce handling to a minimum; and to stimulate scholarly research and increase access through the production of surrogate forms, facsimile publication, microfiche, and computer-stored images.

Studies into the ageing of leathers and the development of a standard method for artificial ageing is another interesting cross-disciplinary collaboration, which in this case has brought together leather technologists, tanners and bookbinders from across Europe. This began in 1991 with a collaborative EEC-funded study under the Science and Technology for Environmental Protection (STEP) Initiative, led by the Leather Conservation Centre in England, into the deterioration of leather. It was subsequently continued by the European Commission ENVIRONMENT Leather project *Deterioration and Conservation of Vegetable Tanned Leather* (1997) and has resulted in an archival bookbinding leather with improved handling qualities.

Learning from other disciplines: developing approaches to conservation thinking

At the cutting edge of research is the application of techniques and theories developed by one discipline to another. The application of economic theory to the quantification and valuation of the preservation of cultural heritage in order to assess the real costs of preservation is an especially exciting new development. This application was pioneered by English Heritage when assessing the impact of different road options at Stonehenge in Wiltshire (Maddison and Mourato, 1998). It was subsequently applied to library and archive materials in research undertaken for the former Library and Information Commission and its successor body, Resource, by Economics for the Environment Consultancy (EFTEC) Ltd in collaboration with the Centre for Social and Economic Research on the Global Environment (CSERGE) at University College London. This study explored the nature of the value of information residing in the recorded heritage and the value of recorded heritage assets themselves. The report sets out a methodology for determining the value of the recorded heritage relating to the notion of economic value, or the individual's 'willingness to pay'. Quantifying the need for preservation is critical in enabling institutions to demonstrate, to politicians and to their own and external funding bodies, the real benefits of preservation (Keene, 1996; Economics for the Environment Consultancy (EFTEC) Ltd, 2000).

The application of risk assessment and management to conservation management is another significant development in collections care philosophy emerging from the museum community, which is equally applicable to libraries and archives. This represents a move away from simplistic measuring of the 'number of items treated' to an examination of the relative potential impact of various agents of deterioration. What is the greatest risk to the collection? Poor security or the state of the roof? Custodial neglect, chemical degradation or catastrophes such as earthquakes, fire and flood? Conversely, what will have the greatest impact on the welfare of the collection (Michalski, 1994; Ashley-Smith, 1999)? The EU-funded Rationalised Economic Appraisal of Cultural Heritage (REACH) project, co-ordinated by Middlesex University for the Building Research Establishment, is developing a method of integrating the different aspects of cost–benefit analysis that can be applied to the cultural heritage and a working prototype management tool, which can be used to evaluate cost–benefit scenarios at different scales. The model is being developed and validated in six practical case studies at sites in the Czech Republic, Portugal, Scandinavia and the UK.

Leading the field

The risk of total loss of digital data when the technology to access it no longer exists underlines the importance of digital preservation. A news item in 2001 makes the point forcibly. Data obtained from Mars by the NASA Viking probes in 1975 contained information on gas released by Martian soils. This was dismissed at the time as meaningless 'chemical activity', but is now thought to provide evidence of microbial life on the planet. However, the electronic data cannot now be read because the tapes containing it are in a format that cannot be read by existing software and thus inaccessible (Krolicki, 2001).

While the museum community has recognized the potential of applying economic and risk theory to preservation, in digital preservation issues it is the library and archive communities that have taken the lead. The electronic arena is notably without boundaries. The development of digital preservation strategies is a prime area for collaboration between cultural institutions, university research departments and, in some cases, software companies and national government agencies.

In response to the loss of early satellite and space data NASA developed the Open Archival Information System (OAIS), which has been adopted by libraries, for example forming the basis of the conceptual data model for Digital Library Systems at both the KB and the BL. The OAIS model is now being turned into a standard by the International Organization for Standardization (ISO) and, with beneficial circularity, the library community is feeding back data to enhance the preservation part of the model. In the CAMILEON project (Creative Archiving at Michigan and Leeds: Emulating the Old and the New), the School of Information at the University of Michigan and the University of Leeds, with funding from the US National Science Foundation and the UK Joint Information Systems Committee (JISC), are investigating the emulation of earlier technology as a digital preservation strategy. Research at the KB in the Netherlands, undertaken in conjunction with IBM, is examining the scalability of emulation. In the UK the NPO has produced a useful synthesis of recent studies on digital preservation (Feeney, 1999).

Features of successful projects

Successful collaborative preservation projects are both practical and transferable. A need is identified, a potential solution proposed, and the collaboration develops a momentum that takes it beyond the initial period of funding. Continuing success is usually driven by one or more visionary individuals or institutions, provided partners continue to be committed.

Collaboration seems to work well for disaster preparedness because the activity is not constant. Resources are pooled and held pending a need that cannot be predicted, but which, when it occurs, requires an immediate response. Collaborative digital preservation works well because everyone is involved in the digital revolution, the technology is constantly changing and advancing and no one yet knows the answers. The NPO-led Preservation Assessment Survey has been taken up because individuals and institutions can see the benefits of assessing their collections and developing their own preservation and funding strategies, while also contributing to the picture of national preservation needs.

Organizational mechanisms

Organizational mechanisms are enabling mechanisms. Collaborative mechanisms are put in place for the general good rather than with specific results in mind. Such mechanisms do not, usually, have a set timescale, but will last as long as there are perceived needs and benefits. Their purpose may also change over time. They include formal groupings such as professional associations, committees and working groups as well as more informal channels.

Information and awareness

To provide a forum for the provision or exchange of information or to raise awareness are common reasons for bringing people and institutions together. The NPO was established by the BL in 1986 in response to the Ratcliffe Report, which highlighted the need for a central source of advice, information and training on all aspects or traditional conservation and preservation, especially for those parts of the library and archive sectors without recourse to specialist preservation and conservation information or personnel (Ratcliffe and Patterson, 1984). This remit was subsequently extended to include digital preservation and, following a review in 1996, a broader funding base was sought. The NPO is currently jointly funded, as a resource for all libraries and archives in the UK and Ireland, by the BL, PRO, the national libraries of Scotland and Wales, Trinity College Dublin, CURL, Cambridge University Library and the Bodleian Library in Oxford. It has recently undergone a further review and is preparing a sustainable business plan for 2002–5. The NPO has had a number of technical panels and committees of experts such as the Preservation Administrators Panel, the Digital Archiving Working Group or the National Committee for Preservation Surrogates, which can be called on for advice. It also provides further mechanisms for the exchange of technical and professional information, as well as a testing ground for the building blocks for a national preservation strategy, such as the Preservation Assessment Survey (Foot, 2001; National Preservation Office, 2001). The UK and Ireland Blue Shield website, launched and hosted by the NPO, provides basic disaster advice.

The UK NPO model has been used in the establishment of national preservation offices in New Zealand, Australia and Argentina. In the Netherlands the National Preservation Office was set up specifically to drive the Metamorfoze initiative (see below). In the USA, the Library of Congress is currently taking the lead in convening a debate on a national preservation strategy.

Training and education

Projects and other initiatives often provide a mechanism for collaborative training and education and the sharing of expertise, especially in the fast-moving field of digital preservation. Recent examples include an international preservation management summer school at the PRO and BL in London in 1999, organized jointly by the PRO and the Ligue des Bibliothèques Européennes de Recherche (LIBER) in conjunction with the BL, the ECPA, University College London and the International Council on Archives (Sanderson, 1999); a series of workshops called 'Managing the Hybrid Library' organized by the e-Lib-funded MALIBU project (Managing the Hybrid Library for the Benefit of Users) and a series of digitization summer schools organized by Glasgow University's Humanities Advanced Technology and Information Institute (HATII).

Staff exchanges, internships and secondments seem to be a less common way of sharing scarce skills and expertise in the UK, though their value is generally recognized as a 'good thing'. This appears to be partly due to inertia and partly to the lack of suitable funding opportunities, though the Sharing Museums Skills Millennium Award Scheme (SMSMA), funded to 2002 by the Millennium Commission and administered by Resource, has made a valuable contribution. SMSMA enables both paid and volunteer staff, including conservators, in museums, galleries, libraries and archives to undertake placements with other organizations. Secondments last between three and eight weeks and grants from £1000 to £6000 are available.

Skills and expertise may also be developed and shared through specific funding programmes, such as the Mellon Microfilming Project, which both increased awareness of preservation microfilming and promoted the use of national standards in the UK. At the international level, a number of organizations are sharing information and resources with others through promotion and dissemination via the internet: for example, the ECPA, NEDLIB, RLG's Preservation Program (PRESERV), the internet-based Cornell 'Digital Imaging Tutorial' and PADI (Preserving Access to Digital Information), the National Library of Australia's gateway to digital preservation resources.

A key aspect of sharing expertise is the transfer of practical conservation and preservation skills from the developed to the developing world. As a very general observation, most successful initiatives seem to entail not flooding a developing area with new technology, often without adequate maintenance or training, but rather promoting the use of local and sustainable materials, and establishing a network of trained local professionals capable of undertaking both conservation and future training programmes. The Prevention in Museums of Africa (PREMA) programme devised by the International Centre for the Study of the Preservation and the Restoration of Cultural Property, Rome (ICCROM), was carried out over the period 1990–2000 with funding from a variety of sources and in partnership with the University of London Institute of Archaeology, the Université de Paris Sorbonne and the Canadian Conservation Institute. The Department of Preservation and Conservation at Cornell University has, with external funding, trained interns from South East Asia and has seconded staff to teach and train in Burma, Cambodia, Egypt, Laos, Thailand and Vietnam.

Bringing people together

People are brought together in project steering and management committees, where a variety of professional and institutional interests and perspectives may be represented. Such committees usually have a limited timespan, but occasionally survive beyond the project, either changing or broadening their remit. The Steering Committee for the Mellon Microfilming Project, for example, is now the National Committee for Preservation Surrogates with a broader remit, which encompasses digital and other surrogates and a sub-committee is advising the Information Services National Training Organisation (isNTO) on the development of national occupational standards for preservation microfilming. People also come together to share information and discuss issues of common interest through a variety of professional and other networks. Professionals keep in touch traditionally through newsletters and meetings, but increasingly through debate on the internet.

Professional organizations and networks include the Society of Archivists' Preservation and Conservation Group and CILIP: the Chartered Institute of Library and Information Professionals' Preservation and Conservation Sub-Committee, the Institute of Paper Conservation (IPC).

International professional organizations and networks include the influential IFLA Core Programme for Preservation and Conservation (IFLA-PAC), LIBER's Preservation Division, the International Institute for Conservation of Historic and Artistic Works (IIC), the International Council on Museums (ICOM), the International Council on Archives (ICA) and the International Conference on Monuments and Sites (ICOMOS).

E-mail discussion lists have revolutionized the exchange of information among conservators and others interested in preservation and conservation issues worldwide, providing a mechanism for instant professional advice, feedback and debate. *Conservation DistList*, run from the University of Stanford is probably the most widely distributed and read (the list archives and other conservation resources are available on the *Conservation OnLine* website at **http://palimpsest.stanford.edu/**). Examples in the UK hosted by JISCmail (the National Academic Mailing List Service) include the recently established National Council for Conservation-Restoration's *Conservation-NCCR* and *Conservation-Research: for those researching the conservation of objects, works of art, buildings etc.* In contrast to many lists that flood subscribers with mail, the *Digital-Preservation Announcement and Information List*, which disseminates information on the work of the JISC Digital Preservation Focus, the DPC and related initiatives, is deliberately filtered to be low-traffic.

Successful organizational mechanisms

Organizational mechanisms for preservation will thrive as long as there are perceived needs and benefits in collaborating. They may survive for the short or long term, but if the need or benefit no longer exists they will wither and die, or reinvent themselves. Steering and management committees are good examples of successful short-term collaborations brought together for a specific task, namely to guide a project. Raising awareness, providing advice, or meeting training needs are longer-term requirements, which are more likely to change over time, especially in response to the emergence of new issues such as digital preservation. The NPO's original focus on traditional preservation, for example, later shifted to encompass microfilming and then digital issues. At the same time, other new groupings have developed specifically to address digital preservation issues such as the DPC (see below). The effectiveness of professional and other networks depends on the will and enthusiasm of the members and their willingness to share and to work together on specific issues of common concern. The success of e-mail discussion lists in enabling the exchange of information may ultimately lead to the disappearance of many traditional newsletters or their rebirth in a new format.

Strategic initiatives

Through strategic initiatives institutions work together to deliver the national and international preservation agenda. Formal and informal links between institutions with shared agendas provide a mechanism for the sharing of information, the discussion of common issues and the development of strategic plans. It is interesting, in this context, that traditional 'boundaries' between preservation and other aspects of collections care, collection management and collection development are becoming less sharp so that collections are being considered holistically. Logically, collections care and collection management include preservation and all of these are intimately linked with collection development. A number of initiatives in the UK are exploring the potential for collaborative preservation.

Making the case

Through the NPO, its funders have made the case for a UK and Ireland preservation strategy for both traditional and digital library and archive materials (National Preservation Office, 2001) and have begun to put some of the building blocks in place (Foot, 2001). This is now being taken forward on several fronts by a variety of organizations and institutional groupings.

Taking the lead

The lead in cross-sectoral and cross-domain issues in the UK belongs with Resource: the Council for Museums, Archives and Libraries, which is about to complete a Stewardship Strategy. This, in conjunction with other strategies for education, information and communications technology and the distributed national collection, will guide and inform Resource's future thinking and planning for collections care and collection management across its constituency. A key role for the Resource Stewardship Strategy will be the co-ordination of the multiple areas of activity and interest across the domains. At government level this is matched by increasing interest in more sophistication in performance measurement, moving from, for example, simple quantification of numbers of items conserved to more qualitative measurement of the impact of the preservation effort on collections, such as the percentage held in appropriate environmental conditions.

Although the concept of the 'distributed national collection', its care and management, embraces all sectors, the lead here is being taken by libraries and archives, especially in the digital sphere. The high level Research Support Libraries Group (RSLG), established in 2001, includes all the national libraries of the UK, together with the major academic research libraries, and has, as part of its remit, the development of a UK-wide strategy for preservation for long-term access as well as investigation of the potential for collaborative storage. With significant funding from the higher education sector, this Group will be in a strong position to translate its strategic thinking into practice. It is not, however, clear how RSLG will relate to the Consortium of University Research Libraries (CURL) Taskforce on Resource Management, set up in 2000, which is to promote the development of national policies and collaborative arrangements among partner institutions for retention, relegation and storage and for preservation and surrogacy. CURL has already taken a lead in digital archiving through its Cedars project, set up in 1998, which is addressing the strategic, methodological and practical issues of digital preservation and providing guidance for all libraries in best practice. Here the major academic research libraries are together addressing a complex issue, which will inform both the digital preservation policy of institutions in all sectors and the national strategy.

Following on from earlier work on collaborative collection development, the Standing Committee on Legal Deposit (SCOLD) of the six copyright libraries in the UK has recently established a preservation group, SCOLD-Pres, with an ambitious remit to facilitate and enable collaborative preservation among its members. If joint programmes are to be achieved, the current co-operative climate offers the best chance of success. The current strategic consultation exercise at the

BL, which points towards a distributed national collection, reinforces this approach. The collaborative approach to mass deacidification mentioned above, if realized, will also form a strand of the national preservation strategy.

The Shared Preservation in Scotland (SPIS) programme aims to share responsibility on a voluntary basis for the preservation and retention of research level collections throughout Scotland. In stage 1, funded by the Scottish Higher Education Funding Council, Dr Janet Gertz, Head of Preservation, Columbia University Libraries, New York, identified the components of a shared preservation programme, and the obligations of participating libraries (1999). Stage 2, funded by the former Library and Information Commission, builds on this work by investigating how a shared preservation programme can most effectively be applied to research collections within a local, regional and national context in Scotland. A shared programme is not yet a reality, but SPIS has all the elements to be truly co-operative and will be watched with interest.

Only one truly nationally enacted strategy for the preservation of cultural patrimony, the Delta Plan in the Netherlands, has worked so far. The General Audit Office advised the Dutch Parliament that an evaluation of the national collections was necessary, because of the significant backlog of objects requiring treatment. In consequence, a rescue plan and a revised cultural heritage policy were launched in 1990 by the Ministry of Welfare, Health and Cultural Affairs. A decision was made not to conserve items in very poor condition, but to spread available resources as widely as possible, so that a little conservation was applied to a large number of items. The programme also resulted in a major training programme (Ashley-Smith, 1999, 312–16). A key reason for success, in this instance, seems to have been ministerial-level impetus and dynamism. Metamorfoze, co-ordinated by the National Preservation Office of the Netherlands, is a follow up surrogacy programme for acidic manuscripts, books, newspapers and periodicals dating from the period 1840–1950.

National digital preservation strategy

Digital preservation particularly lends itself to strategic collaboration and partnership, partly because it is an emerging topic, partly because of its relevance to all sectors, partly because of the refreshing honesty it engenders in the recognition that no one knows the answers and partly because so many interests are alert to the issues and are tackling them in a variety of ways. Significant digital preservation activity and research may, for example, be carried out within broader work programmes such as that of RLG's Digital Taskforce in the USA or the AHDS in the UK.

A feature of digital preservation is that the preservation element of the life cycle management of the digital object has to be addressed right at the beginning. This is the ideal model for the life cycle management of traditional collections and offers the opportunity for improving the life cycle management of traditional collections by analogy. Here it may be more difficult to identify the specific preservation element, but the strength of this approach is that preservation issues are not treated in isolation but as part of whole-collection working. The weakness is that the preservation element can be diluted by other concerns.

In digital issues, the overall lead in the UK will be taken by the Digital Preservation Coalition (DPC), which is to develop a national digital preservation agenda within an international context. A collaborative approach is being taken because it is recognized that the issue of digital preservation is greater than any one institution or sector. The Coalition is envisaged as operating on four levels: co-ordinated activities undertaken individually by member institutions and sectors; core activities of common interest and benefit to all members, supported by resources from the membership; collaborative projects and programmes taken forward with project funding from a variety of sources; and the creation and further development of a national digital archiving infrastructure in the UK. The Coalition was developed during 2001 by a small group of partners, led by JISC and the BL, with a manifesto, constitution, timetable and programme of activities.

Public archives, in particular, have to address the implications of recent initiatives and legislation in the UK intended to create the e-society, such as 'Modernising Government' and the 'Freedom of Information Act'. In libraries, the implications of legal deposit of electronic material are being addressed in projects such as the Digital Library System at the BL, working in parallel with the KB in the Hague (sharing of experience between the two partners is facilitated by a Memorandum of Understanding). A secure network between the UK copyright libraries for the shared use of electronic material is also being investigated. Another interesting initiative is The European Library (TEL) project, in which eight national libraries across Europe are exploring the feasibility of linking existing national digital libraries into a pan-European digital library, accessible to a much wider audience than at present.

A draft Resolution on Digital Preservation from the CDNL was proposed at the United Nations Educational, Scientific and Cultural Organization (UNESCO) General Conference in October 2001. This calls attention to the fact that many of the world's cultural, educational and scientific resources are increasingly produced, distributed and accessed only in digital form and that digital information is highly susceptible to technical obsolescence. It urges member states to take appropriate action for ensuring its preservation. It is hoped that, if adopted, the resolution will help all memory organizations obtain support and financial commitment to tackle the challenge of digital preservation at the national level (van Drimmelen, 2001).

Setting standards

NEWSPLAN and the Mellon Microfilming Project are both good examples of the imposition of national standards through collaborative projects. In the area of digital preservation, where there are, as yet, no national or internationally recognized standards, practitioners are looking to findings and recommendations of strategic collaborations such as the Cedars project and the DPC for direction.

Standards play an important role in promoting best practice, whether in traditional or digital preservation, and are a key strand of national preservation policy. In the UK, their value is demonstrated through: the development and promotion of standards for collections care and the Preservation Needs Assessment; the development of best practice for digital preservation by the Cedars project and the DPC; the use of standards such as BS5454-2000 by archival inspecting bodies such as the PRO and the Historical Manuscripts Commission; and the requirement of funding bodies such as HLF that conservation and preservation projects meet relevant recognized standards.

Conclusion

The elements of success for strategic initiatives are more complex and diverse than for projects and organizational mechanisms. Political considerations play a greater role. If collaboration coincides with the political *zeitgeist*, then co-ordinated preservation activity and funding can result, with attendant standards and training. However it is noticeable how few integrated, national preservation strategies there have been worldwide.

Collaborative preservation projects are easier to organize and execute, notwithstanding the hidden and opportunity costs of co-operation, than strategic initiatives. It is more difficult to carry out core activities, such as the legal duty of care that many institutions have, in collaboration with others, than to mould, define and confine a one-off project. The Oxford Conservation Consortium, whereby seven Oxford colleges contribute to and sustain a conservation facility, is a rare example of successful consortial working to carry out the core activity of collections care.

The compelling logic of defining the national preservation need in order to make the best use of resources chimes with the collaborative *leitmotif* in many parts of the written heritage world at the moment, and by combining the advantage to the individual institution with the greater, altruistic 'good', now is the time to attempt this most complex of preservation partnerships.

References

Ashley-Smith, J. (1999) *Risk assessment for object conservation,* Oxford, Butterworth-Heinemann.

Beagrie, N. and Jones, M. (2001a) *Preservation management of digital materials: a handbook,* London, British Library.

Beagrie, N. and Jones, M. (2001b) *Preservation management of digital materials workbook: implementation in libraries,* BL Co-operation and Partnership Report 10, available at
www.bl.uk/concord/projec15.html

Bell, N. and Lindsay, H. (2000) *Benchmarks in collections care for UK libraries,* Library and Information Commission Research Report 55, London, Library and Information Commission.

Browne, M. (2000) ECPA receives EU grant for photo project 'SEPIA', *NPO Journal,* **6** (April), 4.

Dungworth, N. and Wakeling, W. (1999) A model for assessing preservation needs in libraries, *NPO Journal,* **3** (January), 11–12.

Economics for the Environment Consultancy (EFTEC) Ltd (2000) *Valuing our recorded heritage,* Unpublished report to the Library and Information Commission.

Eden, P. et al. (1998) *A model for assessing preservation needs in libraries,* British Library Research and Innovation Report 125, London, British Library Board.

Eden P. and Gadd E. (1999) *Co-operative preservation activities in libraries and archives: project report with guidelines,* British Library Research and Innovation Report 161, London, British Library Board.

European Commission ENVIRONMENT Leather Project EV5V-CT94-0514 (1997) *Deterioration and conservation of vegetable tanned leather,* Protection and Conservation of European Cultural Heritage Research Report No 6, Copenhagen, Royal Danish Academy of Fine Arts.

Feeney, M. (ed.) (1999) *Digital culture: maximising the nation's investment: a synthesis of JISC/NPO studies on the preservation of electronic materials,* London, National Preservation Office.

Foot, M. M. (2001) *Building blocks for a preservation policy,* London, National Preservation Office.

Gertz, J. (1999) *Development of a program for shared preservation in Scotland (SPIS),*

Scottish Confederation of University and Research Libraries, available at **spis.cdlr.strath.ac.uk/final.html**

Hansen, E. F. and Reedy, C. L. (eds) (1994) *Research priorities in art and architectural conservation*, Washington, American Institute for Conservation.

Jacobs, D. and Brown, M. (2001) Raman spectroscopy: drawing together history, art and science, *NPO Journal*, **8** (April), 8.

Jones, M. (2001) Digital preservation management: a workbook for training, *NPO Journal*, **8** (April), 14–15.

Jones, S. (2000) Preservation needs assessment for archives, *NPO Journal*, **6** (April), 3.

Keene, S. (1996) *Managing conservation in museums,* Oxford, Butterworth-Heinemann in Association with the Science Museum.

Krolicki, K. (2001) *NASA data point to Mars 'bugs', scientist says*, reported on Digital-Preservation Announcement and Information List (3 August), available at **www.jiscmail.ac.uk/cgi-bin/wa.exe?A2=ind0108&L=digital-preservation&F=&S= &P=207**

Maddison, D. and Mourato, S. (1998) *Valuing different road options for Stonehenge*, Report for English Heritage, Global Environmental Change Working Papers, GEC 99-08.

Matheson, A. (1998) NEWSPLAN preserving newspaper heritage, *NPO Journal*, **1** (February), 8–10.

Michalski, S. (1994) A systematic approach to preservation: description and integration with other museum activities. In Roy, A. and Smith P. (eds), *Preventative conservation practice, theory and research: preprints of the contributions to the Ottawa Congress, 12-16 September 1994*, London, International Institute for Conservation of Historic and Artistic Works.

Museums and Galleries Commission (1998) *Levels of collection care: a self assessment guide*, London, Museums and Galleries Commission.

National Preservation Office (n.d.) *Mellon Microfilming Project: final report 1988 to 1997*, London, National Preservation Office.

National Preservation Office (2000) *Guide to preservation microfilming*, London, National Preservation Office.

National Preservation Office (2001) *A national preservation strategy for library and archive collections in the United Kingdom and Ireland: principles and prospects*, London, National Preservation Office.

OCLC/RLG Working Group on Preservation Metadata (2001) *Preservation metadata for digital objects: a review of the state of the art*, available at **www.oclc.org/digitalpreservation/presmeta_wp.pdf**

Porck, H. J. and Teygeler, R. (2001) *Preservation science survey: an overview of recent developments in research on the conservation of selected analog library and archival materials*, Amsterdam, European Commission on Preservation and Access.

Ratcliffe, F. W. and Patterson, D. (1984) *Preservation policies in British Libraries: report of the Cambridge University Library Conservation Project*, BLR&DD Library and Information Research Report 25, Cambridge, Cambridge University Library.

Rhys-Lewis, J. (2001) *The enemy within! Acid deterioration of our written heritage*, BL Co-operation and Partnership Report 8, available at **www.bl.uk/concord/proj99report1.html**

Sanderson, B. (1999) Preservation management summer school 19th-23rd July 1999, *NPO Journal*, **5** (October), 8–9.

van Drimmelen, W. (2001) *Draft resolution on digital preservation*, reported on Digital-Preservation Announcement and Information List (25 July), available at **www.jiscmail.ac.uk/cgi-bin/wa.exe?A2=ind0107&L=digital-preservation&F=&S= &P=371**

7
E-co-operation
Derek Law

The habit of library co-operation

Libraries and librarians have been predisposed towards co-operation since before the word 'electronic' was coined, so it should come as no great surprise that this has provided an almost instinctive motivation when faced with the new challenges of the electronic information environment. Indeed libraries were some of the early adopters of 'new technology' while library automation already has a 40-year history. Perhaps the best examples of this come in standards work, whether classification schemes such as UDC (Universal Decimal Classification) or record exchange formats such as MARC (Machine Readable Catalogue). Such co-operation has fostered the emergence of international interlending and document supply services, a much under-regarded triumph of the negotiating skills and standards work of librarians (Law, 1998).

At local level, numerous efforts have been made to share collection development policies: union catalogues of all sorts remain a typical goal; common staff training programmes are routine; and shared information on journal cancellations is also widespread. Even common access rights for staff, if not students, are steadily spreading. However, there is a feeling that this achieves little but equality of mediocrity. The Research Support Libraries Programme (RSLP) in the UK has recently announced a study into barriers to deep resource sharing, that is, the treatment and management, as a single collection, of the collections of several institutions. As long as collection size remains a powerful symbol for most institutions, it seems unlikely that really deep co-operation will flourish. Unless and until institutions outsource their library collections and services to a third party in the shape of a metropolitan library, it is difficult to see anything other than marginal resource sharing.

Alongside these cautious steps research has become an increasingly collaborative international activity. Studies have repeatedly shown that in the last decade multi-authored papers have grown in number while, at the same time, the number of co-authors from the same institution has steadily declined as a fraction of the total (Lesk, 1999). The first papers with over 1000 joint authors have appeared. Such research must stand on a common base of research knowledge. It can be no coincidence that this has happened at a time when networks and electronic information have expanded, even as most libraries continued the ever gentle decline into discreet but distressed poverty.

The digital revolution seems to some librarians to offer possibilities for avoiding many of the issues that hinder traditional resource sharing. The fear of being swamped by non-institutional users, of resources becoming unavailable to the main user group and of opening hours – all disappear in the great universal 24-hour pond that constitutes the internet. But the reality is inevitably more complicated than the rosy-tinted aspiration. This chapter will look at two types of e-co-operation: first, the use of electronic tools better to manage and share existing, effectively paper-based, resources; second, the sharing of electronic information resources and services that exist only in electronic form. In both cases barriers as well as opportunities exist.

Sharing collections: the barriers

Co-operation has proved possible in the relatively confined world of paper-based libraries. It proves much more difficult in an electronic world with many other stakeholders. Although great progress has been made in areas such as electronic preservation and metadata standards, a whole variety of other issues from network topology to intellectual property rights inhibit the development of truly shared and co-operative endeavours. The most fraught area, perhaps because it is the newest, is that of new 'born digital' material. Libraries, on the other hand, continue to make progress where electronic tools are used to foster the sharing of existing paper resources.

One difficulty lies in the still incomplete state of catalogues. The *Full disclosure* study estimated that the number of items still requiring retroconversion in libraries was 50 million (Chapman, Kingsley and Dempsey, 1999). The Library and Information Commission, which commissioned the report, has now been replaced by the government agency Resource. This body has an expanded remit covering museums, archives and libraries, but, from my perspective, as yet little apparent interest in engaging with this or other major library issues. Other agencies are attempting to fill this vacuum and a more recent study undertaken for the British Library (BL), the Joint Information Systems Committee (JISC) and RSLP has proposed the creation of a national union catalogue (Stubley, Bull and Kidd, 2001).

This seems likely to go ahead, at least in the serials area, where records are notoriously poor.

The BL has also taken a recent and more positive approach to sharing. Its Co-operation and Partnership Programme seeks to create groupings locally and regionally as well as nationally. It is funding a number of studies and projects with this in mind. At a more strategic level the Higher Education Funding Councils have joined with the national libraries to set up a strategic review group looking at the future of collections and access to them nationally, including preservation issues (Smith and Milne, 2001). It is intended that this group will expand to cover the public library sector, thus taking on some of the strategic role abandoned by Resource.

Another interesting consortial approach, which claims to be about collection sharing – although it appears to have more to do with interoperability and access – is The European Library (TEL) project. This links the national libraries of Finland, Germany, Italy, the Netherlands, Portugal, Slovenia, Switzerland and the UK with the Instituto Centrale per il Catalogo Unico in Italy and the Conference of European National Libraries (CENL). With a grant of 1.2 million EUR, the project will make recommendations on interoperability, while the partner libraries are all committed to making digital collections available at the end of the pilot stage. The libraries use different standards for cataloguing, indexing and preserving materials, and reaching a consensus on the way ahead will be no small task.

Electronic journals and the revolt of the academy

Commercial electronic products can be inimical to resource sharing. Once paper materials had been purchased by a library they were available to all. While the same can be true of consortially purchased materials, electronic products bought by single institutions can have very restrictive licensing conditions, which prevent non-members of libraries from using them. The definition of library and indeed university and other membership institutions is blurring. Although co-operatives have operated in metropolitan areas for many years with a whole panoply of acronyms from BRASTACS (Bradford Scientific, Technical and Commercial Services) to CALIM (Consortium of Academic Libraries in Manchester), this has tended to operate at a fairly superficial level ranging from staff training to reciprocal access. Deep sharing of collections, which allows the material in a group of libraries to be treated as a single entity, has not really happened. There are many possible reasons for this, varying from the statutory to institutional rivalry. However, a number of studies were commissioned in 2001 to explore these issues and to find the real nature and extent of the problem. The results will be awaited with interest. The position has not been helped by the commercialization of information and its consolidation into an ever smaller number of major media conglomerates on the one hand, and a deeply hostile set of attitudes to what were seen as reactionary and restrictive practices by libraries on the other.

For some time concern has been expressed by librarians over the cost of journals in general and the price, terms and conditions associated with electronic journals. One of the first attempts to address this was the formation of the Scholarly Publishing and Academic Resources Coalition (SPARC). With the motto 'returning science to scientists' it set out to create a new stable of attractive low-cost scholarly journals, which aimed to use technology to cut costs and promote access. It has grown steadily, and opened a European office in 2001 to try and spread the benefits of cheaper journals more widely (ACOSC, 2001).

There is a marked and growing dyspepsia with electronic journals. Despite the hype they can remain difficult to use. One study found that 55% of the e-journals in its sample could not be accessed on the first attempt, with more than half the failures due to problems with the journals themselves, while about one-fifth of the journals had incomplete archives (Harter and Kim, 1996, 454). In the UK the first National Educational Site Licence Initiative (NESLI) deal with Academic Press included an agreement that, should the deal not be renewed, the files would be archived with the community. In the event, this has happened and the community is left not only with a huge file with no obvious home, but also with an incomplete file since the publisher has felt unable to provide any of the images or tables for copyright reasons – thus one suspects rendering the file practically unusable.

One of the most encouraging features in 2001 has been the awakening of the scientific community from its torpor on the future of scientific communication. A recent letter in *The Guardian* correspondence columns raged against 'scientific feudalism' as practised by major STM publishers (Lankester, 2001). The Public Library of Science is a groundswell activity initiated by Varmas, the originator of PubMed Central. Some 23,000 scientists in over 160 countries have signed the petition, which declares that, from September 2001, the signatories will publish only in journals that offer free access to their published articles six months after publication and which have their (biomedical) articles archived in PubMed Central. Whether or not this initiative succeeds, huge progress has been made in that thousands of academics and not just librarians recognize a major issue to be addressed.

The Open Archives Initiative and e-print servers

For some time a small band of zealots, led by figures such as Paul Ginsparg and Stevan Harnad, has argued for the creation of public domain archives of scientific research. These initiatives were typically based on the concept of large, international, centralized but discipline-based sites. After several years during which this attempt to break the dominance of commercial publishing over scientific research has seemed to have a limited effect on commercial scientific publishing, the Open Archives Initiative (Van de Sompel and Lagoze, 2000) has given the concept a new lease of life, although now with a burgeoning of institutionally based e-print servers. Essentially, the Initiative offers interoperability and cross-platform searching for electronic pre-prints. Such servers are typically managed by libraries and, since this co-operative activity relies on the adoption of common standards rather than the creation of common facilities, it may have greater prospects of success.

Co-operation, funding and charging

Co-operation between different library sectors is an inescapable way forward. Such working is not, of course, new. For many years Library and Information Plans (LIPs) have played a much neglected part in trying to foster co-operation. They have, however, proved rather static and need increasingly to look at much deeper levels of resource sharing as well as sharing information about resources. Yet over much of the country, shared and publicized access, at least for reference use, would represent a significant step forward in local co-operation. New technologies have made some ambitions simpler and more accessible than hitherto, for example local websites linking OPACs are now a realistic possibility. This can operate either at the simple but effective level of the M25 Group linking higher education libraries within the area ringed by the M25 London Orbital Motorway, or at the deeper level of the Co-operative Academic Information Retrieval Network for Scotland (CAIRNS) project, which allows cross-platform searching.

Co-operative acquisition and shared purchase are two other somewhat traditional and possibly neglected activities. In British higher education the practice for the last decade has been to seek national site licence deals, a practice begun by the Combined Higher Education Software Team (CHEST) on behalf of the Funding Councils and latterly carried out by NESLI. While NESLI deals have become less and less attractive – for a variety of reasons – there has been a separate growth of interest in regional cross-sectoral deals based on the Metropolitan Area Network (MAN) structure. Areas as disparate as the west of Scotland and the West Midlands have begun discussions with publishers on deals of this nature. Most of the agreements to purchase specialized material, whether organized by subject or date, seem to have fallen into desuetude. However, projects such as the GAELS project based at Glasgow University (Glasgow Allied Electronically with Strathclyde: Information Environment for Engineering) seem to imply a renewed interest in deep resource sharing.

National deals have been characteristic of the 1990s, but even as their acceptability appears to be diminishing in the UK, countries such as Canada are embarking on this process with major national initiatives. In essence, such deals offered publishers little but reduced income in return for reduced sales and reduced administrative overheads. Major publishers are beginning to approach regional deals rather more eagerly, since these open up the possibility of increasing income by adding new groups such as schools to a consortium, thus obtaining at least some income from sectors where full price sales would prove impossible.

Perhaps one desirable funding model for national negotiating agencies would be to provide national templates for regional deals. There seems little merit in each region of a country spending large amounts of time negotiating individual contracts, given that information on terms and conditions will quickly spread round the system. It seems at least theoretically possible that pricing based on a formulaic model could be negotiated nationally. This would allow regional consortia to determine which constituent groups will accept a deal and use the formula to calculate the cost without the need for protracted and expensive negotiations.

Regional trading companies and consortia, based on MANs, are beginning to emerge in the UK. Hitherto the MAN structure has been dominated by technical considerations. However, as they become settled structures there is much more interest in how they can be used effectively. The cross-sectoral state-wide consortia common in the USA, or in Australia, such as Co-operative Action by Victorian Academic Libraries (CAVAL), are beginning to be looked at with interest.

Local digital libraries are the most interesting way of bringing together a range of cross-sectoral resources. The Glasgow Digital Library is one such model. Although funded by the RSLP programme of the Funding Councils, it is a cross-sectoral project including public, further education and higher education libraries, which has set out to create a completely new library in Glasgow with access to new resources of relevance to the entire local population. Other such libraries are being planned: there is as yet no single standard model that is emerging, although the concept of collections free at the point of use does appear to be an important basic requirement. Similar developments are beginning to emerge in the West Midlands and the north east of·England.

Decisions on what to include may be facilitated by the more relaxed attitude of publishers to intellectual property rights. Organizations as varied as the British Medical Association, Elsevier and the Association of Learned, Professional and Society Publishers have all eased restrictions on authors, generally allowing them to post individual articles on local websites. It does not take much thought to see the output of local authors as a key building block of local digital libraries. Conversely, some publishers such as Elsevier, an undoubted industry leader, remain wedded to the notion of fixed access points (your PC in your office), apparently flying in the face of the trend towards more mobile computing devices (Wissenburg, 2000).

Universities and e-universities

Of course most libraries are part of larger organizations. The nature of these parent organizations is also changing dramatically in the face of globalization, with co-operation an increasingly prominent phenomenon, both encouraged and enhanced by the development of networks. One example of this can be seen in the massification of higher education.

Universities in the west of Scotland tend to be thought of as local universities: 40% of their student intake comes from within 35 miles. Strathclyde University has about 20,000 students, 15,000 of whom come from the heartland of Scotland. That is the traditional core business, but the University is branching out in all sorts of ways. Increasingly, and typical of the sector, it is a global university. There are a further 40,000 students who come to the University for an examinable qualification every year, bringing the student base to 60,000 people. These students come from over 100 countries, some of them in residence and some of them working abroad doing sandwich courses of various sorts, as well as many people from the surrounding area seeking to update their skills or develop new ones. The university market has been globalized. Strathclyde University is a typical example, with such arrangements as a business school in Shanghai, shared degrees based in Malaysia, where pharmacy students undertake two years of training and then come to Scotland for their third year, and a European Masters degree in business, jointly awarded by four universities, in which the students take modules at four different universities across Europe. This is very different from the sort of university of even a decade ago.

The same blurring is true locally. Strathclyde has a joint postgraduate law school with the University of Glasgow, joint social work and journalism departments with Caledonian University, and some joint nursing degrees with Bell College. It is very difficult to say where the boundaries of the University stop. When one comes to issues like site licensing of journals, this raises the interesting issue of what constitutes a site. Students increasingly work away from the University. Building programmes in universities have not kept pace with expansion. We rely on *de facto* distance learning, on students not turning up at the University for significant periods of the week, because there is nowhere to put them. We rely on students studying in residence halls and at home. Anybody who has tried to use a modem from home with its wonderful 56 kilobyte capacity will understand why many students prefer to go to the growing number of community learning centres with broadband technology and broadband capacity.

Students will continue to study close to home. They will be undertaking legitimate study in libraries that are not part of the institution. At the same time, a typical university will have hundreds of staff and students off-site who legitimately wish to gain access to the resources that have been purchased and paid for. The concept of the university being a bounded physical place in which students work and study has disappeared.

There has been a growth in the concept of e-universities. Not only has this been seen as a way for existing universities to broaden their student base, but it has also been recognized as a commercial opportunity for new companies. Consortia of universities, such as Universitas 21 and the European Consortium of Innovative Universities, have appeared internationally while, in countries such as the Netherlands and the UK, national initiatives have been launched. Commercial providers started well and those like the University of Phoenix have earned excellent reputations. However, the market has proved tougher than expected. Pensare, the e-learning company that developed the technology for the Duke University MBA Cross-Continent programme, has filed under Chapter 11 of the US bankruptcy laws in the light of the general financial freeze facing dot.com companies. Unext, one of the major companies in the field, has reduced its educational operations. Quisic (formerly University Access) has withdrawn from education to concentrate on the corporate market because of lack of funds, thereby affecting plans for courseware development both at the University of North Carolina and at the London Business School. FTKnowledge, part of the Pearson Group, has also been moving away from standalone e-learning products. All this reflects the fact that the market is developing much more slowly than enthusiasts predicted (Bradshaw, 2001).

Nevertheless, the growth of shared web-based courses seems inexorable. Even if this were not likely for commercial reasons, both the UK Higher Education Funding Councils and the European Union (EU) have set aside massive funding to promote such developments. Inevitably, this will involve libraries in activities ranging from the creation of some parts of courseware, such as reading lists with hotlinks to texts or other resources, to the preservation and cataloguing of the courseware itself.

New opportunities for libraries

Hitherto, most electronic co-operation between libraries has concentrated on the mechanization of traditional and well understood practices: shared or consortial library systems; shared or co-operative acquisition of commercial products; and shared work on standards. We have now moved to the brink of exploring innovative forms of co-operation.

Co-operative digitization

Much writing, ranging from nostalgia to scare-mongering, has either predicted the death of the library in the digital environment, or tried to open up new avenues of activity (for example Lombardi, 2000). This tends to be on the lines of Lesk's view that 'libraries must focus on access and service, not buildings and volumes' (Lesk, 1999, 261). Such thinking is predicated on the growth of commercial rivals ranging from search engines to publishers. In reality, search engines can only ever be as good as the cataloguing of the resources, and there has been a consistent tendency to ignore the unique, the ancient and the public material that represents much of a library's acquisition and work, and which will rarely be taken up by the commercial sector. Therefore, a growth in interest in collectively created public sector and semi-commercial resources is a very welcome development. Projects such as the Scottish Cultural Resources Network (SCRAN), which open up cultural resources from museums, galleries and archives as well as libraries, have been much admired. The £50 million set aside by the New Opportunities Fund (NOF) for the digitization of resources has brought together a large number of cross-domain consortia, which will produce enormous quantities of digital content from the public sector. This has the potential to be the most enriching feature of e-co-operation. Rare and inaccessible materials from all over the UK will be made universally accessible, either free or for nominal sums. Although the scale of such digitization is remarkable, other major multimillion pound programmes, notably in the higher education sector, have already digitized substantial collections under both the Non-formula Funding (NFF) programme and the RSLP. 'Born digital' collections are rarer. One project looking to develop this is the Scottish University Libraries SAPIENS (Scottish Academic Periodicals: Implementing an Effective Networked Service) project, which is exploring the creation of Scottish scholarly journals online. Other projects to catalogue material in some detail, such as the ScoRe (Search Company Reports) project, which is creating a national catalogue of company reports, represent real 'added value' to users.

International co-operation and time-shift

Most co-operation is based on some kind of geographical contiguity; although some sectoral or subject co-operation has taken place, it has always been limited. An interesting new area of co-operation has emerged thanks to time-shift. The London School of Economics in the UK and Macquarie University in Australia have announced a joint 24-hour IT support service (details available at **www.lse.ac.uk/itservices/help/Helpdesk/rehds.htm**). Others are known to be examining similar initiatives for library reference support. This offers exciting possibilities for the provision of services, 24 hours a day, seven days a week, to users who will increasingly operate in different times and spaces from the physical library with its typical 12-hour opening period.

There are many international co-operative projects, notably in the field of digitization, but these tend to be limited in scope and content. Lesk has noted that, whereas commercial publishing ventures concentrate on full-text, fairly complete and often image-free resources, library material is scattered, mimics exhibitions, is heavy on pictures and light on text. He suggests that, by concentrating on little-used, out of copyright material, libraries may avoid all the issues to do with intellectual property rights, but offer collections that are of little interest (Lesk, 1997). This is perhaps an over-cautious view. On the one hand, the act of assembling scattered materials into a coherently available collection makes the material more useful while, on the other hand, there is much evidence that the very act of digitizing or cataloguing into an OPAC greatly increases use of previously neglected material.

Information arbitrage

Very little effort appears to have been made by librarians to explore the concept of information arbitrage. Users show a surprising naïvety when faced with the internet. There is a simplistic assumption that, because it is easy to find answers on the internet, such answers are correct. There is also a tendency to assume that resources are both comprehensive and based in North America. Thus has grown the group for which Plutchak has coined the mellifluous phrase 'the satisfied inept' (Plutchak, 1989). Although the inadequacy of search engines is almost a commonplace, it has come as a shock to many to discover how partial they are. Search engines have come under proper scrutiny and a study in 1998 showed, rather to everyone's surprise that they addressed only a fraction of the then estimated 720 million web pages. Coverage varied from a best of 34% for Hotbot to a worst of 3% for Lycos. Within that range, up to 5% of links were 'broken' although 'pages that timed out were not included in these statistics' (Lawrence and Giles, 1998). Less remarked has been the concept of cybercolonialism. One of the best examples of this is the History Channel's series on the mid-19th century war between the northern and southern states of the USA called 'The Civil War', which is shown throughout the world, apparently assuming that there has only ever been one civil war in one country.

Much co-operative library resource has gone into the creation of portals, which attempt to identify relevant and appropriate resources and provide some degree of quality assurance. However, all this effort is aimed at assessing the quality rather than the availability of sites. Indeed the whole issue of the evaluation of digital libraries and digital information remains at the stage of identifying terminology and concepts (Saracevic, 2000). No discussion appears to have taken place on whether a form of the Pareto Principle (the 80–20 rule) might be relevant: in other words, is a 'perfect' site available only 20% of the time superior to a less complete site available 80% of the time? It is a commonplace in Europe that North America becomes a virtual country in the afternoon as local traffic grows and slows response times to unacceptable levels. Identifying and providing access to mirror or alternative sites to the East rather than the West may provide better quality responses. In commercial terms, seeking to purchase access to off-peak resources on the other side of the globe should be explored. There is a substantial opportunity for librarians to explore improved access to independent, authoritative and accurate information.

Conclusion

To paraphrase Ranganathan: the development of electronic media and new forms of co-operation among libraries creates an environment where there is a role for the provision of the right information, in the right format, at the right price, for the right user, at the right time (Ranganathan, 1967).

References

ACOSC Digest of Scholarly Communication News (2001) posted on LIS-SCONUL (1 June).

Bradshaw, D. (2001) A bankrupt idea's great future, *Financial Times,* (28 May), 9.

Chapman, A., Kingsley, N. and Dempsey, L. (1999) *Full disclosure: releasing the value of library and archive collections,* LIC research report 10, London, Library and Information Commission.

Harter, S. P. and Kim, H. J. (1996) Accessing electronic journals and other e-publications: an empirical study, *College & Research Libraries,* **57** (5), 440–456.

Lankester, A. (2001) Letter, *The Guardian,* (28 May).

Law, D. (1998) Access to the world's literature: the global strategy, *Library Review,* **47** (5/6), 296–300.

Lawrence, S. and Giles, C. L. (1998) Searching the world wide web, *Science,* **280** (5360), 98–100.

Lesk, M. (1997) *Practical digital libraries: books, bytes and bucks,* San Francisco, Morgan Kaufmann.

Lesk, M. (1999) The organization of digital libraries, *Science & Technology Libraries,* **17** (3/4), 9–25.

Lombardi, J. V. (2000) Academic libraries in a digital age, *D-Lib Magazine,* 6 (10), available at
www.dlib.org/dlib/october00/lombardi/10lombardi.html

Plutchak, T. S. (1989) On the satisfied and inept end user, *Medical Reference Services Quarterly,* **8** (1), 45–8.

Ranganathan, S. R. (1967) *Prolegomena to library classification,* 3rd edn, Bombay, Asia Publishing House.

Saracevic, T. (2000) Digital library evaluation: toward an evaluation of concepts, *Library Trends,* 49 (2), 350–69.

Smith, G. and Milne, R. (2001) Towards a national strategy for research support, *Library Association Record,* **103** (7), 417–18.

Stubley, P., Bull, R. and Kidd, T. (2001) *Feasibility study for a national union catalogue,* prepared for the Joint Information Systems Committee [by the University of Sheffield], available at
www.uknuc.shef.ac.uk

Van de Sompel, H. and Lagoze, C. (2000) The Santa Fe Convention of the Open Archives Initiative, *D-Lib Magazine,* **6** (2), available at
www.dlib.org/dlib/february00/vandesompel-oai/02vandesompel-oai.html

Wissenburg, A. (2000) The future of journals publishing?, *ISS newsletter – BUS,* Issue 3, available at
www.kcl.ac.uk/depsta/iss/cit/news/newsletter/issue3/fjp.html

8

Joined up funding: promoting and facilitating collaborative work

Ronald Milne

Introduction

In recent years in the UK considerable sums of money have been made available for library, archive and related projects. One of the sectors that has been particularly fortunate in this respect is higher education – the university sector. This chapter will focus on funding that has been available in that sector and, in particular, through the Research Support Libraries Programme (RSLP), an initiative funded by the UK Higher Education Funding Councils. RSLP has encouraged collaboration principally between higher education libraries and archives, but also between the higher education sector and libraries and archives in other sectors including, notably, the British Library (BL). Consideration will be given to the challenges facing funders in achieving strategic objectives in a political climate in which cross-sectoral, and even cross-domain, activity is encouraged by central government, but where the existing formal funding structures and mechanisms do not necessarily assist in achieving those objectives. The successful actions taken by some funders to join up funding streams, so that cross-sectoral ventures can be resourced, are described. I conclude that, if the library profession is serious about cross-sectoral library activity, it must convince central government that the provision of substantial, properly joined up funding is an imperative that cannot be ignored.

Why collaborate?

Why collaborate? There is one simple and compelling reason: no library is now able to meet the existing and potential information needs of all its users. Closer co-operation and partnership in the library and information domain is essential if we are to reduce unnecessary duplication of effort, optimize the use of financial and other resources, extend provision in areas not previously or fully covered and provide value for money across the publicly funded UK library system as whole. There is another, more mercenary, reason for working together, and that is that central government and funding agencies such as the New Opportunities Fund (NOF), the BL and RSLP, recognizing the myriad of advantages in collaborative working, are greatly disinclined to fund single institution proposals. Librarians who ignore this reality, perhaps believing that their library is a special case, are likely to find themselves investing a great deal of time in writing proposals for which there is no return.

Bottom-up collaboration

Traditionally, librarians have had a good record of co-operating in informal ways, and in the past bottom-up approaches have often succeeded in stimulating collaborative activities which have resulted in improved services for users. Sometimes this has involved *ad hoc* arrangements between a small number of libraries and the relatively modest cost has been hidden within libraries' budgets. Some consortia, such as the Consortium of Academic Libraries in Manchester (CALIM), the Scottish Confederation of University and Research Libraries (SCURL) and the Consortium of University Research Libraries (CURL) are subscription organizations and are consequently in a position to employ staff and deploy the remaining resource. Having funds assists such organizations in the pursuit of their missions, but, without doubt, the success of many collaborative activities depends in large part on the energy of individuals, whether they are salaried employees or representatives of member institutions. Such energy may be directed into securing additional finance from funding agencies, and a number of consortia have been able to advance their work, whether on a pilot or practical basis, by securing external funding. 'Co-operation in the spirit of enlightened self-interest', one of the governing principles of CALIM, no doubt partially articulates the *raison d'être* of many library consortia.

The need to act nationally and strategically

Consortia are, however, unable themselves to effect truly significant strategic change at a national (UK) level. This is for two main reasons. First, because none of the consortia, even those such as CURL whose annual membership fees are quite substantial, can themselves contribute the sums of money that would be required to effect a significant course of action. One obvious illustration of this situation is that the COPAC, the union catalogue of the CURL libraries' holdings, which has certainly been of great benefit to the academic community, would not exist, at least in its present form, without substantial financial input from the Higher Education Funding Councils' Joint Information Systems Committee (JISC). Second, librarians are not their own controllers. They are, rightly, accountable to their employing institutions, and tensions can arise between institutional interests and consortial missions. In short, they themselves are not really able to commit their institutions, and therefore their libraries, to long-term policies or courses of action.

It is my belief that step-shifts in most strategic matters are really only achieved when funding is made available through the targeted injection of substantial sums of money into the system. In UK universities in the past (and in the foreseeable future, although there have been murmurs of discontent), these sums of money have been found by top-slicing higher education budgets, so that particular programmes or services can be funded. Perhaps the most high profile example of the success of this approach is the Joint Academic Network (JANET, or SuperJANET4 in its current incarnation). This world-class network was set up in the mid-1980s to link all UK universities. It was, and is, funded through top-sliced funding and it is almost inconceivable that this development, which has had such obvious benefits for the academic community, could have been funded in any other way. When it comes to 'buying in' to such services, or to initiatives such as the Electronic Libraries Programme (e-Lib) or RSLP, there are always likely to be major players whose participation is required to make a service or a project a success, but who either believe they cannot afford to take part, or who think they probably might be able to do the job better themselves. It would seem to me to be much better that the nation's higher education budget is top-sliced, for the Common Good.

The Follett and Anderson Reports and top-sliced funding

The Follett Report (1993), which was the first major review of higher education libraries for 25 years, was instrumental in securing significant sums of top-sliced funding – a total of more than £115 million – for UK university libraries. One outcome of the report was that £50 million was provided by the Higher Education Funding Councils for a capital programme, which helped extend, refurbish and re-equip library buildings. Another £50 million was spent in funding the Specialised Research Collections in the Humanities initiative (also known as 'Follett' or 'NFF' – an abbreviation for 'Non-Formula Funding'), which ran from 1994 to 1999, and £15 million was invested in the first two phases of the e-Lib Programme, which ran from 1995 to 1998 (Rusbridge, 1998). A further £4.1 million was made available for a third e-Lib phase (ESYS, 2001).

Like the NFF initiative and the e-Lib Programme, the origins of RSLP also lie in the Follett Review but, as importantly, in the associated Anderson Report (1996).

The Anderson Report grew out of the concern of the Follett Committee that, in the face of major changes in the funding and research aspirations of UK higher education institutions, and also in the context of major innovation in library technologies, there was both a need and an opportunity to improve organizational arrangements and the capacity of UK libraries to support research, especially, though not exclusively, in the humanities and social sciences (Anderson, 1998).

Crucial to securing the £30 million of top-sliced funding for RSLP was the urge for increased collaboration and sharing in the use of the research infrastructure proposed by the report of the National Committee of Inquiry into Higher Education, (Dearing Report, 1997) and the report of the associated Scottish Committee (Garrick Report, 1997). In the eyes of some key policy makers, library collaboration and access were seen as a testbed for wider access arrangements envisaged by these reports (Anderson, 1998).

The Research Support Libraries Programme: joining up libraries

The Anderson Report was wide-ranging, covering not just higher education, but also relationships between higher education and the BL, the other legal deposit libraries, the libraries and resource centres of the UK research councils, and the important libraries funded by learned and professional societies (Anderson Report, 1996, para 12) and, not surprisingly, the Research Support Libraries Programme has promoted the concept of 'joined up libraries' since its inception.

The Programme's principal aim is to facilitate the best possible arrangements for research support in UK libraries. The programme is 'managed' – interventionist – and it attempts to take a holistic view of library and archive activity throughout the UK (Milne, 2001). The Anderson Report had recommended a programme of collaborative collection management activities, based on networks of library holdings, with the object of moving towards the concept of distributed national collections in particular groups of disciplines or types of materials. The concept of distributed national collections of library research resources (the 'distributed national collection', or 'DNC') promoted by the Programme has achieved a strong acceptance in the library community, and collaborative cross-sectoral work that will contribute to its development is now featuring on the agenda of other funding agencies. A major thrust of the initiative has been to encourage higher education institutions to work consortially and with the national libraries, other research libraries and public libraries in order to move towards this vision. This has very often presented us with a practical challenge, as RSLP monies may only be applied within the higher education sector. I shall discuss this matter in detail below.

Access

Mapping and co-ordinating collections and their acquisition, cataloguing, subject-indexing and preservation is only worthwhile as part of a national strategy if readers who need access can obtain it (Anderson, 2000), and even if we uphold the concept that libraries should be free at the point of use, most of us would acknowledge that there are costs attached to service provision for users who are not members of the 'home' institution. Libraries with major holdings within the UK higher education sector have until very recently received no compensation for the 'burden' imposed by visiting research-active staff and students from other UK higher education institutions.

An access funding arrangement is perceived to have a number of advantages. It reinforces and puts on a sounder footing the presumption of open access for researchers across the whole higher education library system, changing a potentially withdrawable privilege into a right; and the scheme rewards holding libraries that have made extra efforts to be hospitable to external readers.

The RSLP Access strand seeks to compensate the libraries for extra costs incurred in providing access and services for 'external researchers'. As there were no comprehensive and auditable data already available in the late 1990s, RSLP commissioned the first large-scale survey of the use made of UK higher education libraries by external researchers. Almost 5000 research-active staff and students were surveyed. The work involved measuring the number and, where appropriate, the length of in-person, e-mail, letter, fax and telephone contacts that researchers had with libraries other than those of their own institution. It also asked respondents to list the top five UK higher education libraries in terms of importance for research in their discipline(s). The survey confirmed that there is very extensive use of libraries beyond those of the 'home' institution and provided the data on which the RSLP Access strand annual allocations for the academic years 1999–2000 to 2001–2 were made (Milne and Davenport, 1999).

A small number of research libraries outside the higher education sector have made the point that, as they provide significant support to higher education researchers, they too should have a share of the RSLP access funding. This is a valid observation but, as I have noted above, the current funding regime does not allow transfer of monies from the higher education sector to other sectors.

RSLP projects, partnership and commitment

RSLP projects are mainly dealing with traditional library materials but, in almost every case, creating an electronic resource. These take the form of bibliographic and archival records, collection descriptions, digitized images and texts, and web directories and portals.

Most of the projects funded by RSLP are discipline oriented, although one or two focus on a format. The Programme is concerned with material that is of value to research, wherever it is held, whether in one of the major research libraries such as Oxford University's Bodleian Library or the John Rylands University Library of Manchester, or in the libraries of one the newer universities, such as those of Manchester Metropolitan University or London Guildhall, or in a library outside the higher education sector. There are as many as 21 partners in a consortium. Several projects are multifaceted and are working in a number of Programme areas.

In common with other funding programmes, partnership funding, sometimes known as matching funding, was required by RSLP for certain types of activity. For example, funding from institutions was required for all retrocataloguing and cataloguing and indexing elements in projects; the Programme's contribution was no more than 70% of approved project costs. In other Programme activities, RSLP looked favourably on demonstrable financial commitment by institutions. In the case of one of the largest projects, which seeks to provide enhanced access to collections of 19th century pamphlets in CURL libraries, CURL itself demonstrated its corporate commitment to the activity by making a significant financial contribution.

Academic fields in which RSLP projects are expected to have a strong impact include archaeology, art history, art and design, business studies, geography, history, non-European languages and area studies, the performing arts, theology and church history, veterinary science and women's studies. The research community as a whole will benefit from projects that seek to map research collections in UK regions: RASCAL (Research and Special Collections Available Locally) is recording resources in Northern Ireland, while a project led by the University of Wales, Aberystwyth, is mapping the library and archive resources of the Principality. Among other activities, SCONE (Scottish Collections Network Extension) is identifying research collections in the newer universities as well as in other higher education institutions in Scotland and is extending the Research Collections Online database to include information relating to them. There are major collaborative collection management projects for Asian studies and for Russian and East European studies, and projects that seek to facilitate access to such diverse materials as pamphlets, aerial photographs, early manuscript and printed maps of Scotland, cartoons and architectural drawings. More detailed information relating to RSLP projects may be found on the Programme website at **www.rslp.ac.uk/**.

Clearly, there is no point in funding project activity if the most senior university managers do not support involvement, or where institutional commitment to a particular academic discipline is not 100%. It is absolutely necessary, too, to identify a single individual who will take ultimate responsibility for the general direction of a project and management of project funds. It is certainly helpful if that person has a close understanding of library and other information matters, and has something to lose if a project goes awry. Proposals to RSLP were, therefore, required to identify a lead higher education institution that would be responsible for the management and delivery of the project or study. All submissions had to name a single, senior, institutional officer, such as the university librarian or archivist of the lead institution, who would have responsibility for the management of the supported project. Proposals also had to be accompanied by a brief statement of support from the vice-chancellor, principal or director of each higher education and other organization.

Among the non-higher education partners participating in RSLP projects are the BL, the National Library of Wales, the National Library of Scotland, the National Archives of Scotland, the Public Record Office, the Brighton and Hove Museum and Art Gallery, English Heritage, Glasgow City Council Libraries and Archives, the Royal Commission on Ancient and Historic Monuments of Scotland, the Tate, the Wellcome Institute and Westminster City Archives.

Cross-sectoral funding?

Many colleagues have asked how we can really begin to fulfil the vision of a distributed national collection in particular groups of disciplines or types of materials when RSLP can fund only higher education institutions. Where it has been possible, some institutions, such as the BL and the Royal College of Physicians of Edinburgh, realizing the potential for the Common Good, have funded their own participation in RSLP projects. However, the number of organizations in this enviable position is small. Other institutions have been able to devote some staff time to projects, again very often because they recognize that participation is to the benefit of their own users as well to the broader research community. In many cases RSLP has funded project infrastructures, both organizational and technical, that have allowed institutions outside the higher education sector to take part at relatively modest cost.

While I would contend that RSLP has promoted a holistic view and encouraged collaborative cross-sectoral work because it is the sensible thing to do in library terms, ready acceptance of the need to work together, and the vision of a distributed national collection has almost certainly been expedited because the time is ripe. The political messages have been very clear. I have already referred to the Dearing and Garrick Reports (1997) and the urge for increased collaboration within the higher education sector. In 1998, the UK Department for Culture, Media and Sport (DCMS), recognizing the regional bias of the public library system, remarked that regional structures in the UK vary greatly in their effectiveness, and that their relationship with regional cultural bodies could be improved. The Department proposed 'to develop a stronger regional library structure encouraging all libraries within a region to work together' (DCMS, 1998). More recently, a Library and Information Commission Education and Libraries Task Group report, *Empowering the learning community* (LIC Education and Libraries Task Group, 2000), took the view that closer cross-sectoral co-operation within the library domain would ensure better support for lifelong learners and result in managed access to academic libraries in a way lifelong learners have not had before. Notably, the report recommends that cross-sectoral funding arrangements should be established. The creation of Resource: the Council for Museums, Archives and Libraries in April 2000 sent a clear signal that collaboration between the domains was encouraged, if not expected. An additional impetus has been provided by the active pursuit of a national information policy for the UK, where a shared vision of the way ahead is of great importance, and where barriers that exist between constituent parts of the information community need to be broken down (Law, 2000).

While the current political climate is such that cross-sectoral and even cross-domain collaboration is encouraged, when it comes to funding, government departments are perhaps not yet as joined up as we might wish. In England, for example, three government departments control the funding of most of the institutions that host research collections. The Department for Culture, Media and Sport allocates funds to the BL. The Department for Education and Skills provides the funding for the higher education sector, working through the Higher Education Funding Council for England, which is accorded a fair degree of autonomy. The Department of the Environment, Transport and the Regions allocates the funding to local authorities, which then determine how much is spent on public libraries. Different arrangements apply in Northern Ireland, Scotland and Wales (British

Library/Higher Education Task Force, 2001a). In my view, such arrangements for the disbursement of library funding have in the past led to a 'silo' mentality where cross-funding between sectors, for example from higher education to national or public libraries, is generally forbidden.

Consequently, it has been important to find means whereby different funding agencies can themselves act collaboratively. There is a great deal of challenge funding available in the UK at present, for example, from RSLP, from the British Library's Co-operation and Partnership fund, or from the Heritage Lottery or New Opportunities funds. In as far as different funders are very often attempting to achieve somewhat different strategic goals, it has been important to find some common ground. However, we noted previously that the library profession has a good record of co-operation, and I can attest to a desire on the part of my colleagues to arrive at pragmatic outcomes, if at all possible. In discussion, the aims of different funding programmes, criteria for funding projects, synchronicity of resource streams, and possible mechanisms for co-funding or providing complementary funding for cross-sectoral projects have been taken into consideration and we have met with some success.

The RSLP 'Charting the Nation' project, for example, is co-funded by the Scottish Cultural Resources Area Network (SCRAN). The project is providing sophisticated electronic access to digitized early manuscript and printed maps of Scotland, and associated material. Partners in the project include a number of university libraries in both Scotland and England, and also the Royal Commission on the Ancient and Historical Monuments of Scotland, the Royal Scottish Geographical Society, the National Library of Scotland and the National Archives of Scotland. The participation of the organizations outside the higher education sector is crucial to the success of the project and SCRAN funding has facilitated their involvement. SCRAN will have access to the 'Charting the Nation' digitized images and other data and, by agreement, the material will be repackaged for SCRAN use.

RSLP and BLCPP: cross-sectoral collaboration for project funding

RSLP has enjoyed an amicable and fruitful relationship with the BL Co-operation and Partnership Programme (BLCPP) since its launch in 1999, following the BL's 1998 strategic review and consultation exercise. The BL's desire to work collaboratively at the coalface had already been demonstrated by an indication of its desire to work together in projects that were successful in bids to the first RSLP call for proposals and it was making internal funding available to support project work in the appropriate collection areas.

The agendas of the RSLP and the BL programmes have different emphases, but both organizations wish to promote collaborative cross-sectoral working. In the BL's October 2000 call for proposals, work with the higher education sector was highlighted and the BL indicated its wish to encourage and enable institutions outside the higher education sector to build on and work with existing initiatives in RSLP and other higher education programmes. The BL welcomed proposals from non-higher education institutions to take part in and extend existing RSLP projects. Joint proposals from higher education and non-higher education institutions for new projects were also welcomed. Where proposals have been of considerable interest to both programmes, arrangements have been made such that RSLP contributes funding that allows higher education partners to participate in a project while the British Library contributes the funding for non-higher education involvement. This has meant that bids have had to meet the criteria of two separate funding agencies. Seven cross-sectoral projects have been funded in this way. Examples include Management of Access to Grey Literature Collections (MAGiC), led by Cranfield University; a National Art Library-led project to create a union list of serials for art, architecture and design; and Co-East Plus, a project led by the Co-East consortium based in Cambridgeshire Libraries, which will facilitate access to the resources of libraries in the public, academic and health sectors throughout the east of England. This project and 'Cecilia', a project led by the International Association of Music Libraries (UK branch), which is mapping the nation's music collections, has Resource: the Council for Museums, Archives and Libraries as a very welcome third funder.

By funding a series of complementary proposals, RSLP and the BL have also been able to fund the whole of BOPCRIS, the British Official Publications Collaborative Reader Information Service, based at the University of Southampton. This large-scale project aims to save researchers valuable time and effort finding relevant British Official Publications published between 1688 and 1995, by providing a web-based bibliographic database, which enables them, from their own desktops, to:

- search and browse for relevant documents without having to visit libraries to consult hardcopy reference tools
- read abstracts, and view detailed, consistent, subject-indexing of key documents so they can assess whether they need to see the full document
- find out the nearest location of relevant documents, if they decide they need them

• read the digitized full-text version of a limited number of documents.

Within the BOPCRIS framework, the BL is funding work that focuses on material from the period 1688 to 1800 while, as the result of successful bids to two separate calls for proposals, RSLP is funding work covering resources from the period 1833 to 1983 and the periods 1801 to 1832 and 1984 to 1985.

Information about BLCPP and the projects it is funding may be found on the BL's Library Co-operation Website at **www.bl.uk/concord/**.

Further joined up funding

Unlike preceding library and information funding programmes such as NFF and e-Lib, which reported to JISC, the Research Support Libraries Programme reports directly to the UK Higher Education Funding Councils, through a steering group chaired by Professor Michael Anderson. Although RSLP funding decisions are taken completely outwith the JISC framework, it would be something of an indictment of UK higher education if RSLP and appropriate parts of JISC did not establish a rapport and seek to work together on matters of common interest. I am pleased to acknowledge the immense goodwill shown by the JISC Committee on Electronic Information (JCEI) and by the e-Lib and the Distributed National Electronic Resource (DNER) programmes, in particular. Common, or complementary, interests have led to the joint funding of studies such as HILT (High Level Thesaurus) and work that will examine the many human resource aspects of programme and project work. A three-way funding partnership between RSLP, JISC and the British Library funded the feasibility study for a national union catalogue (Stubley, Bull and Kidd, 2001), and the trio are jointly funding further preliminary work that will furnish an implementation plan and a specification of requirements for the development and provision of a serials union catalogue (SUNCAT).

The collection description work undertaken for RSLP by the UK Office for Library and Information Networking (UKOLN) aimed to enable projects funded through the programme to describe collections in a consistent and machine-readable way. This activity has gained some considerable momentum: the Collection Description Focus service based at UKOLN is also jointly funded by the RSLP, JISC and the BL. In addition, these funders are contributing to a scoping study, which is examining how best to create a single searchable repository of collection descriptions, either manually or by automatic harvesting, and the technical and business aspects of running a collection description service. The study is being undertaken by Manchester InforMation & Associated Services (MIMAS), one of the UK higher education national data centres.

The joint funding of projects by higher education and the BL has demonstrated a new willingness and ability to work together to a common end that has not been consistently evident in the past. There is now also unanimity on the need for a shared strategic vision and agreement on the need to build a framework for future sustainable and effective collaboration. Running in parallel with the joint funding arrangements described above, which have largely been initiated and implemented at programme level, the BL and higher education are also working at a higher strategic level to secure better co-ordination of library and information provision and the more efficient use of limited public resources.

The British Library/Higher Education Task Force: a cross-sectoral agenda

Significant developments at a strategic level were first realized in September 1999 when, following discussion between John Ashworth, Chairman of the British Library Board, and Sir Brian Fender, Chief Executive of the Higher Education Funding Council for England, a high-level joint task force was formed with the purpose of identifying areas for future collaboration. At the first meeting, it was agreed that there was a mutual interest in ensuring more effective and efficient overall provision, and each organization agreed to fund jointly work and investigations towards this end, with the Higher Education Funding Council for England and the BL each contributing £50,000 to fund joint studies and investigations.

The Task Force commissioned four studies in total, addressing the following matters:

- mechanisms for co-ordinating the development of the distributed national collection of research resources – known simply as 'the DNC study' (British Library/Higher Education Task Force, 2001a)
- the relationship between the BL's and higher education libraries' objectives, leading to the development of high level performance measures of the BL's contribution to the higher education sector
- the long-term future of the 'legacy collections' of the BL's Document Supply Centre and of higher education institutions, and potential stakeholder relationships associated with them
- the collaborative storage of library resources (British Library/Higher Education Task Force, 2001b).

The Task Force also took a close interest in other areas in which the BL and higher education were working together, for example where higher education programmes and BLCPP were already jointly funding strategic studies, such as the union catalogue feasibility study, or services such the national focus for collection description work. It also noted the development of the BL's *zetoc* electronic table of contents service and contributed financially to the review of the National Preservation Office. The Task Force completed its work in Spring 2001 and an overview report summarizing the outcomes and recommendations of the studies went forward to a new, high level strategic body, the Research Support Libraries Group. The detailed reports were also made available (Smith and Milne, 2001).

The Research Support Libraries Group

The Research Support Libraries Group (RSLG) was formed in order to progress the collaborative agenda for research support provision and provide a suitable national framework for collaboration. It is chaired by Sir Brian Follett and it had its first meeting in July 2001. Members of the Group include senior members of the library profession and of the academic and research community. The remit of the new body, in general terms, is to advise the Higher Education Funding Councils, the British Library and the national libraries of Scotland and Wales on strategies for promoting collaboration in the development and provision of library collections, their long-term management, and services to support research.

The terms of reference for the Group presage a very broad agenda: among other matters, it is expected that the new body will review the operation of the RSLP Access model and recommend options for a long-term scheme to support integrated access to resources of national importance; consider further development of a co-ordinated strategy for, and provision of, materials in printed and electronic form; and assess how best to use the resources of JISC and the DNER team to facilitate this strategy. The Group may also deliberate on how the development and implementation of the framework and mechanisms for a DNC might be funded, and what governance mechanisms might be required. The development of a UK-wide strategy for preservation, with a particular focus to support research and scholarship, is also being considered. As well as receiving the outcomes of the studies undertaken by the British Library/Higher Education Task Force, the Group is commissioning further specialist work in support of its agenda, including an investigation of the need for electronic infrastructure to support 'e-science'.

The Group's work will be carried out over a period of 15 months. Its aim is to produce a strategic vision that will ensure UK researchers have world-class access to research materials, on paper or in electronic form. The body will make recommendations for structures and actions to achieve the vision, and for a funding mechanism to ensure that the changes are delivered (Smith and Milne, 2001).

Conclusion: future funding infrastructure and mechanisms

The formation of such a group is a very positive step in itself and it will be interesting indeed to learn what funding arrangements and infrastructure RSLG proposes for the future. The Group is focusing on strategy for higher education and national libraries and there seems a real possibility – because libraries in these sectors do have a very close mutual interest in research support and have increasingly been working together – that there will be significant practical outcomes resulting from the Group's deliberations. If there is a desire to realize the vision of a distributed national collection, it is to be hoped that the Group will recommend the establishment of an office to lead the activity and commission the work that would be required to progress the agenda. Such an office might act as a facilitator and broker, liaise with those responsible for e-collections, be an advocate for DNC-related activity, and also function as a hub for dissemination (British Library/Higher Education Task Force, 2001a). A continuation and extension of RSLP-type access funding would be a necessary complement to DNC activities. But will RSLG wish, or be able, to consider activity beyond higher education and the national libraries? And if we are to draw libraries in other sectors into DNC-related work, how would a substantial programme of cross-sectoral work be funded, and where would the access money come from?

I referred earlier to the silo-like arrangements we have for funding libraries in the UK, and the difficulties of applying, say, higher education monies to fund work in other sectors, even when the benefit is for those in higher education. The success of the current, rather *ad hoc*, arrangements for co-funding cross-sectoral projects and services really depends on the goodwill of the funding agencies, their committees and officers. We can continue to co-operate in this way, and much will still be achieved; but, in the future, collaborative cross-sectoral work will be regarded as the norm, not because it is politically correct, but because it makes sense. If we take a holistic view of UK library resources and examine the ways in which we can provide an efficient and effective service, cross-sectoral working often emerges as the best vehicle for delivery. It is surely time for the library profession to attempt to persuade politicians and high-ranking civil servants, either that the infrastructure and mechanisms for funding libraries in the UK should change or, at least, that the central provision of substantial funds, administered independently of any sector, could underpin cross-sectoral activity in a manner that would be of benefit to all. Joined up libraries require joined up funding!

References

[Anderson Report] (1996) Joint Funding Councils' Libraries Review, *Report of the Group on a National/Regional Strategy for Library Provision for Researchers,* available at
www.ukoln.ac.uk/services/elib/papers/other/anderson/

Anderson, M. (1998) *The new funding councils' research support strategy.* Paper presented at the Joint Information Systems Committee, Committee on Electronic Information Library Strategy Workshop, Manchester, 30 April–1 May.

Anderson, M. (2000) Anderson Report – origins, vision and current developments, *Relay,* **49**, 4–6.

British Library/Higher Education Task Force (2001a) *Co-ordinating the distributed national collection of research resources: report to the Research Support Libraries Group,* British Library/Higher Education Task Force, available at
www.bl.uk/concord/pdf_files/blhe-dnc.pdf
[A distilled and revised version of 'Mechanisms for co-ordinating the development of the distributed national collection of research resources' undertaken for the Task Force by Nick Moore and Margaret Wallis.]

British Library/Higher Education Task Force (2001b) *The collaborative storage of library resources,* British Library/Higher Education Task Force, available at
www.bl.uk/concord/pdf_files/blhe-colstor.pdf
[A study led by CAVAL Collaborative Solutions and undertaken for the Task Force by Steve O'Connor, Andrew Wells and Mel Collier.]

[Dearing Report] (1997) National Committee of Inquiry into Higher Education, *Higher education in the learning society,* available at
www.ncl.ac.uk/ncihe/index.htm

Department for Culture, Media and Sport (1998) *The comprehensive spending review: a new approach to investment in culture,* London, Department for Culture, Media and Sport.

ESYS (2001) *Summative evaluation of phase 3 of the eLib initiative: final report,* Guildford, ESYS plc.

[Follett Report] (1993) Joint Funding Councils' Libraries Review, *Joint Funding Councils' Libraries Review Group: report,* available at
www.ukoln.ac.uk/services/papers/follett/report/

[Garrick Report] (1997) National Committee of Inquiry into Higher Education, *Report of the Scottish Committee*, available at
www.leeds.ac.uk/educol/ncihe/scottish.htm

Law, D. (2000) Information policy for a new millennium, *Library Review*, **49** (7), 322–30.

Library and Information Commission Education and Libraries Task Group (2000) *Empowering the learning community*, London, Library and Information Commission.

Milne, R. (2001) Enhancing access and progressing the collaborative agenda: the UK Research Support Libraries Programme. In Lynden, F. C. (ed.), *Advances in Librarianship*, **25**, Sidcup, Academic Press.

Milne, R. and Davenport, G. (1999) The Research Support Libraries Programme access survey, *New Review of Academic Librarianship*, **5**, 23–40.

Rusbridge, C. (1998) Towards the hybrid library, *D-Lib Magazine*, **4** (7/8), available at
www.dlib.org/dlib/july98/rusbridge/07rusbridge.html

Smith, G. and Milne, R. (2001) Towards a national strategy for research support, *Library Association Record*, **103** (7), 417–18.

Stubley, P., Bull, R. and Kidd, T. (2001) *Feasibility study for a national union catalogue*, available at
www.uknuc.shef.ac.uk
[A study undertaken for JISC, RSLP and BLCPP and led by the University of Sheffield.]

9
The international dimension
Graham P. Cornish

The nature of international co-operation and partnership

Given that there appears to be a considerable number of opportunities for co-operation, it seems a good idea to begin a chapter on the international dimension by asking just what is meant, if anything, by co-operation in an international context. Perhaps there is no such thing, in which case this chapter could be a very short one!

Co-operative initiatives in a national context frequently, though not invariably, grow out of political, economic or cultural environments. These often come about as a result of government initiatives, which provide the impetus for organizations to work together, either to reduce the impact of negative resourcing or to exploit funding made available to meet specific political goals. They can also be proactive where institutions identify elements in government agendas that they feel they could advance by working together with other players in their particular field. Naturally there must be some benefit to the institution taking part – nobody can afford to be completely altruistic in the modern information world.

Are any of these reasons applicable to the international world? The reply will vary, depending on whether a truly global situation is contemplated or a more regional view is appropriate. In the case of the truly global situation it has to be admitted that essentially the answer is 'no'. Clearly there is no truly global political agenda. Countries and regions have their own aims and objectives, which they will pursue. Despite numerous international organizations exhorting individual nations to make certain issues their priority, many will pay them little more than lip-service as there exist few incentives to follow the guidance set by such well-meaning but often ineffective bodies. While failure to follow a national policy may leave an organization isolated or falling behind its competitors, this is rarely an issue internationally. For example, national government may make funds available to universities that are prepared to develop modern methods of communication to facilitate document delivery and resource sharing. Those who do not wish to co-operate miss out on the installation of advanced telecommunications systems and wider access for their students while limiting the scale of their acquisitions programmes. Internationally there are numerous exhortations to co-operate in document delivery systems, but the only true incentive to do so is either the need to generate revenue for supplying libraries by charging for access to their collections, or to increase access to materials for researchers without significantly increasing the need for more foreign currency. In international terms, the only real power to implement a policy comes from the refusal to fund projects or initiatives that do not meet the criteria set out by the funding body. Thus the World Bank may require certain financial measures to be put in place. UNESCO has the goal of improving the education of women as a major element in its funding programmes, but countries not sharing this goal do not lose anything but simply do not benefit from some additional funding. While this may seem a cynical view of international co-operation, it is nevertheless true that the very nature of partnerships across frontiers is different from those forged nationally.

Despite this somewhat dismal view of international co-operation it would be quite wrong to say it does not exist. What is important is that it exists in a quite different *milieu* from many co-operative ventures that are national in character. How then does international co-operation come about and what are the incentives to promote it?

The international context

In most national situations the information world is divided up both geographically and by area of interest or sector. In addition, the LIS community will be further divided between libraries, archives, information providers, museums and galleries or domain. This is reflected in the structure of many national professional bodies. In the UK, for example, CILIP: the Chartered Institute of Library and Information Professionals has branches serving all geographical areas of the UK and also special interest groups covering such wide-ranging issues as health, community services, rare books and cataloguing. Working together often receives its impetus either from identifying local needs or as a result of particular requirements in a specific sector. Both of these facets are emphasized within the international information community. A number of international bodies working in the LIS field are, in effect, aggregates of national organizations, which have formed an international association of one kind of another. This is, in itself, a form of international co-operation of some significance. It may also be worth noting at this point that there are signs that the focus of international work is increasingly moving away from particular domains to a more integrated approach, so that libraries, archives, museums and other players in the so-called 'cultural' field are identifying more areas of mutual interest.

International organizations

Probably the most concrete expression of international co-operation is the existence of a number of international organizations in the LIS field in its broadest sense. Most of these exist on very limited budgets provided by each of the national associations or institutions that belong to them. They are the most permanent embodiment of international co-operation available. Most function as non-governmental organizations (NGOs), which gives them much greater political freedom than operating as an arm of government. Before its virtual demise in 2000, the International Federation for Information and Documentation (FID) had been in existence for over 100 years and the International Federation of Library Associations and Institutions (IFLA) celebrates its 75th anniversary in 2002. It would, however, be misleading to cite only the two NGOs working in the distinctive library and information field. The International Council on Archives (ICA), the International Council on Museums (ICOM) and the International Council on Monuments and Sites (ICOMOS) all contribute to the wider information scene at the international level.

These organizations often have a small headquarters with only two or three permanent staff. They are supported by large numbers of volunteers who undertake a wide range of activities, partly in work time and partly at their own expense, to further their interests in specific areas of the LIS profession. Given that there is often no measurable benefit to the member organizations, the maintenance of international bodies such a IFLA and FID really does demonstrate a willingness to co-operate internationally. Here is a clear example of all those participating putting something into the partnership and having at least the potential to get something out of it. It is in the nature of things that some people will put in a great deal and others will contribute very little. Conversely, some will benefit a lot, while others will sometimes question what real benefit is obtained from membership. As the funding for some of these bodies comes from the subscriptions levied on individuals by the member organizations, it is essential to have the support of the ordinary members who may otherwise vote to spend their hard-earned cash in other ways. The majority of professional members in any national association rarely become involved in international matters. The contribution by the membership association is therefore a two-edged sword: on the one hand members will ask what the value is of contributing to an international organization but, equally, this gives an opportunity to demonstrate the value of international work to the membership at large.

Fostering co-operation?

Given that the organizations just discussed are themselves examples of co-operation and partnership, it seems reasonable to ask if they, in turn, foster co-operation or provide the environment within which co-operation can flourish. One view is that a few enthusiastic members have an idea for which they obtain some funding and then persuade or cajole relevant libraries or other institutions into participating in whatever project is being arranged. This model is certainly true in some situations and most people who have been involved in any professional body will recognize the symptoms of 'projectomania'. Such personal enthusiasm should not be underestimated, since from time to time it can result in very useful work being carried out. Its greatest disadvantage is that it does not usually have the wholehearted support of the institutions that are members of the NGO concerned. It can therefore be seen as a personal quest to achieve some particular goal, or as being even slightly eccentric in character. Without the sustained support of the institutions concerned such initiatives, however well meant, usually fail to achieve anything permanent. A further benefit of this enthusiasm, however, is that it may well be cross-sectoral in character. Most professional associations that rely on personal involvement are structured to meet the interests of those working in specific areas. The enthusiast may well cross those frontiers where formal approaches cannot. In this respect they mirror the structures of national associations. International associations may equally be geographical in character or emphasize particular subject interests such as music (IAML – the International Association of Music Libraries, Archives and Documentation Centres), art (ARLIS - the Art Libraries Society) or technological universities (IATUL – the International Association of Technological University Libraries). A recent IFLA project managed to bring together people from the sections on bibliography, cataloguing, document supply and collection management.

There are also a number of more specialized international organizations in the field of librarianship that set out to foster co-operation and partnership rather than actively undertake it. The important work in facilitating that essential element in co-operation – networking – must not be underestimated. Examples include IAML, which currently has about 2000 individual and institutional members in some 45 countries throughout the world. Its basic aims are to promote international co-operation and to support the interests of the profession. In fact one of IAML's most important contributions is less in the field of library co-operation than in library information provision. As a major sponsor of several international bibliographies in various aspects of musicology, it plays a vital role in the bibliographic network. A number of other organizations exist in this category, all working in a similar way.

Work carried out by these bodies naturally varies according to their size, interests and capabilities but, broadly speaking, can be characterized in the following ways.

Doing it themselves

In some circumstances the appropriate international body will actually carry out some work using its own resources, developing a project, programme or system on behalf of all its members. It could be argued that this is not true co-operation or partnership but, given the argument made earlier that these organizations are a real example of international co-operation, this can hardly be a valid point of view. Projects and systems managed by the NGO itself are, therefore, a good example of international co-operation carried out in a delegated context.

The IFLA voucher scheme can be seen as one example of this type of co-operation (Gould, 1995). In brief, the scheme is designed to remove some of the financial barriers to international document supply and interlibrary loan. Libraries buy vouchers, which are currently worth $8 each, an amount usually recognized as the average cost of an interlibrary loan transaction. The vouchers are sold from a central point operated by IFLA, which takes responsibility for the financial and administrative aspects of the scheme and also the liability in the event of the scheme failing. A library (library 'A') buys vouchers and then sends them with an international interlibrary transaction to the library from which the loan or photocopy is requested (library 'B'). Library B keeps the voucher as a form of payment and can then send the voucher on to yet another library (library 'C') in the same way. Inevitably, some large libraries receive more vouchers than they can use and so they eventually return these to IFLA where they are redeemed for real money. The scheme is used by nearly 700 libraries in more than 40 countries and continues to grow rapidly. It requires an element of co-operation by individual libraries in that they must be willing to accept the vouchers as a form of payment, but otherwise it is essentially a scheme run by IFLA on behalf of its members. Despite the apparent vicarious nature of the co-operation, nevertheless it requires a general consensus of approval for the scheme and acceptance of it as a meaningful contribution to library co-operation. A positive outcome of the scheme, as well as removing high banking and transaction charges from international document requests, is that it has created a worldwide network of libraries that use the scheme and are enthusiastic for it. As one of the great hurdles to any form of international co-operation is the overcoming of apathy, this is itself a major contribution to the international library scene.

A further good example is the International Standard Bibliographic Description (ISBD), prepared by the Working Group on the General International Standard Bibliographic Description set up by the IFLA Committee on Cataloguing. The various ISBDs for different types of material are still produced and updated by the IFLA Universal Bibliographic Control (UBC) Programme in Frankfurt. As a result of their international standing, the second edition of the *Anglo-American cataloguing rules* (AACR2, 1998) is based on the ISBD general framework for the description of library materials, including the order of elements in the catalogue entry and prescribed punctuation. Similar work has been carried out for archives by the ICA (International Council on Archives, 2000).

Funding others to do the work

NGOs do not always have either the time or expertise to carry out some of the work they would wish to do and therefore it is appropriate to find others to do it on their behalf. An interesting example of this is the creation and maintenance of the Universal Decimal Classification (UDC). The organization now known as the International Federation for Information and Documentation was founded to manage UDC and had performed that function since its origin around the turn of the last century. During the 1980s, however, it became clear that a more broadly based, and financially autonomous, organization was needed to administer and exploit UDC; as a result FID, together with the publishers of the Dutch, English, French, Japanese and Spanish editions, became founder members of a new body, the UDC Consortium (UDCC). The Consortium assumed ownership of UDC on 1 January 1992 and one of its first actions was to create an international database that could be the source of many kinds of UDC edition. This database is called the Master Reference File (MRF), and is held at the Royal Library in the Hague, updated once a year. The UDCC has also appointed an editor-in-chief and an editorial board with international membership to oversee the content of UDC and contribute to its revision. UDC is undoubtedly recognized as a worldwide tool for library classification and information management. Its content and structure are determined by the Consortium but its decisions can, and are, influenced by those who use the scheme and as a result there are several UDC user groups around the world. The very fact that UDC has become an international standard means that it has brought together not only libraries, but also computer experts, classification experts, scientists and publishers to work more closely to achieve a global standard in this sphere. Nevertheless, FID found that its 'baby' had grown to the point where it needed to leave the parental home and become independent. FID was wise enough to allow this to happen, a decision that has given the scheme an independence while still acknowledging its origination with FID. This example clearly demonstrates the way in which international co-operation can lead to the creation of a major contribution to information development, without the need for the original NGO to continue to be involved.

Being funded by others

The opposite model from that just described can also frequently be found in international circles. NGOs rarely have the resources to carry out all their work themselves and often rely quite heavily on other organizations for funding. This usually takes the form of undertaking research or project work for the other organization that is consonant with the aims and objectives of the NGO itself. A good example, which also serves to demonstrate other areas of international co-operation, is the UNESCO Memory of the World Programme. The first objective of the Programme is to ensure the preservation, by the most appropriate means, of documentary heritage of world significance and to encourage the preservation of documentary heritage that has national and regional significance. A twin objective is to make this heritage accessible to as many people as possible, using the most appropriate technology, both inside and outside the countries in which it is physically located. Preservation of the documentary heritage and increased access to it complement one another. Access facilitates preservation and preservation ensures access. For example, digitized materials can be accessed by many people and demand for access can stimulate preservation work. Another element of the Programme is to raise awareness in the Member States of their documentary heritage, especially of aspects of that heritage that are significant in terms of a common world memory. To achieve some of these goals UNESCO set up a committee to advise on the planning and implementation of the Memory of the World Programme, which makes recommendations on raising funds and on allocating such funds to projects. It also makes recommendations on placing elements of the documentary heritage on the Memory of the World Register and granting the Memory of the World label to selected projects. Specifically, the statutes of the committee require co-operation with appropriate international NGOs such as ICA and IFLA. IFLA has major programmes in both the areas of maximizing access to information, for example, the Universal Availability of Publications (UAP) Programme and also in preservation and conservation, so that the UNESCO programme is actually advancing and supporting the aims of IFLA itself. At the same time ICA also has a major involvement in preserving and recording the archival heritage of the world so that, again, its own objectives are furthered by working with UNESCO on this programme. A great deal of the survey work and information gathering for the Memory of the World Programme was carried out by ICA and IFLA.

This major worldwide project demonstrates the point that NGOs may take forward their own agendas by fulfilling the needs of other bodies prepared to fund the work, but it must be remembered that there are many much smaller projects that rely on the same formula.

Stimulating others

A major part of international co-operation is helping others to see the possibilities of a situation and encouraging them to exploit it in the light of experience from elsewhere. Much of the value of international co-operation is in improving national situations about which international organizations can rarely do much to help. However, most NGOs carry out work of an advisory, teaching or training nature to achieve these goals. Frequently run on very limited budgets, such workshops and seminars will often be staffed by volunteers, sometimes released by their employers, but working in their own holiday time. Their aim is to show LIS professionals, government officials, funding agencies and educators just what can be done to improve the services provided. Most of the core programmes of IFLA run workshops on topics such as preservation, professional development, improving access to information and government information and freedom of expression. Their catalytic action can, and occasionally does, encourage governments and other policy-making bodies to put libraries and access much higher up their agenda than was formerly the case.

Working together

If the work that an NGO does can be considered a form of international co-operation, how much more should co-operation between NGOs be seen as international co-operation *par excellence*. Although in the past there was a certain mutual exclusivity between FID and IFLA, this has largely been dissipated by the virtual demise of the former, caused mainly by financial difficulties. However, co-operation between the NGOs in the field is increasing. The most concrete and comprehensive example of co-operation is the establishment of the International Committee of the Blue Shield (ICBS). Its aim is to provide authorities and professionals with expertise and networks in the case of armed conflict or natural disasters that could affect cultural heritage. New kinds of conflicts that have broken out in recent years and serious natural disasters, such as the floods in Florence in 1966, in Poland in 1997 or the fires in St Petersburg or Los Angeles, to quote just a few, have led four non-governmental organizations (IFLA, ICA, ICOM and ICOMOS) to found the ICBS, which has taken up the emblem of the Hague Convention for the Protection of Cultural Property in the Event of Armed Conflict. The four organizations are also working together to co-ordinate risk-preparedness at an international level and to encourage it at a local level. So far, national committees have been set up, or are being set up, in Belgium, Canada, France and the Netherlands. An interesting and highly relevant development from this initiative has been the establishment of a United Kingdom and Ireland Blue Shield Organisation (UKIRB), which was launched in March 2001. This is an example of what is itself an international committee growing out of an international initiative taken by four NGOs.

Instability and inertia

There are a number of international organizations that might be expected to have dynamic programmes to encourage co-operation but which fail to do so. One example of an organization that might be expected to generate co-operation but does so only occasionally is the Conference of Directors of National Libraries (CDNL). The IFLA voucher scheme was given a kick-start by CDNL, which gave the idea its general support and persuaded one member to provide seed money to start it up. Given that CDNL members were not asked actually to *do* anything else this could hardly be called international co-operation! Subsequently, CDNL members were asked to provide funding for the continuation of the project, which they did voluntarily and somewhat haphazardly. The reasons for such patchy support is that organizations like the CDNL rely very much on the enthusiasm of individual people who are members. The hopes for a perfectly good project can be dashed by the intervention of one member with powerful influence. A change in personnel can lead to a complete change in attitudes – for good or bad! One facet of international co-operation never to be ignored is its instability. In fact, this must be one of the few concrete examples of co-operation that CDNL has actually achieved. Mostly the Conference meets annually to exchange views and set up working groups to study specific issues, but rarely engenders any co-operation to *achieve* anything concrete.

Individual initiatives

It would be quite wrong to assume that all international co-operation is under the aegis of international organizations. There are numerous examples of co-operation and partnership between individual libraries in different countries, although these are often *ad hoc* and rarely have any long-term future. One example of reasonable longevity and stability is the Joint Steering Committee for Revision of the *Anglo-American cataloguing rules*. The Joint Steering Committee develops and maintains the *Anglo-American cataloguing rules* according to established principles for bibliographic description and access in support of effective cataloguing practice. To this end, the Committee works to formulate a cataloguing code that is responsive to user needs and to changes in the information environment, and that results in cost-effective cataloguing. The constituent organizations represented on the Joint Steering Committee are the American Library Association, the Australian Committee on Cataloguing, the British Library, the Canadian Committee on Cataloguing, CILIP: the Chartered Institute of Library and Information Professionals and the Library of Congress. In this case there is co-operation between national libraries, library associations and national bodies, which are themselves examples of national co-operation.

Perhaps one of the most notable international initiatives, largely driven by a few enthusiasts for the benefit of the many, is the International Coalition of Library Consortia (ICOLC), which first met informally as the Consortium of Consortia (COC) in 1997. The Coalition continues to be an informal, self-organized group comprising (as of September 2000) nearly 150 library consortia from around the world. The Coalition serves primarily higher education institutions by facilitating discussion among consortia on issues of common interest. It now also contributes to library–publisher discussions on licensing issues and helps inform those trying to negotiate site and consortia licences throughout the world.

In fact the role of professional associations in developing programmes of co-operation and partnership is an important one. Very often the national association is the best way into developing individual partnership programmes. The American Library Association (ALA) has a long history of international work and has provided specialists to help in both developing and developed countries with specific problems.

However, it would be wrong to characterize all international co-operation as on the grand scale, arranged by bodies with international status. At the other end of the spectrum are schemes such as that for interlibrary loan co-operation between libraries in Mexico and the USA. Informal in one sense, it facilitates direct lending between these libraries without any major formalities and has worked well for a number of years (Morales Campos, 1994).

Regional and local co-operation

It would be reasonable to assume that the regional picture regarding co-operation might be a series of microcosms of the international one. However, the patterns and nature of regional co-operation vary considerably round the world and no general remarks can be made. As the region of the world where co-operation is most highly developed is Europe, this will be the focal point for looking at regional activities and the yardstick with which to compare and contrast any other regional initiatives.

It must be said immediately that the term 'Europe' is being seriously misused in the press, the media and even professional literature. There is a tendency to work on the equation 'Europe = the 15 Member States of the European Union' and leave the other 18 or so countries out in the cold. For this reason 'Europe' will be used here to indicate the traditional continent and 'EU' will be used to show initiatives from the European Union.

The Council of Europe

The only organization that operates throughout Europe as far as cultural matters generally are concerned is the Council of Europe. Although the Council has sponsored various pieces of research and held a number of conferences and seminars, there is little direct co-operation or partnership being encouraged. The emphasis in the Council of Europe is very much on the book and publishing industry rather than on libraries *per se.*

Conference of European National Libraries (CENL)

Unlike its global equivalent, CENL is very active in encouraging co-operation among its members. The primary example is Gabriel: Gateway to Europe's National Libraries, which is the world wide web service for Europe's national libraries represented on CENL. There are currently 40 national libraries from 38 Member States of the Council of Europe participating in CENL and Gabriel. Gabriel's mission is to provide information about Europe's national libraries, in particular about their collections and their services, in order to facilitate access to them, and to foster the development of new services based on a shared infrastructure. To achieve this, it serves as a comprehensive and up-to-date online guide to the functions, collections and services of Europe's national libraries and promotes them in every appropriate way. Significantly, one of its objectives is to support the building of collaborative links between European national libraries in the networking field.

Among the common tasks of the national libraries are the setting up of national deposits for printed and electronic publications and the compilation of national bibliographies. National libraries are seen to represent the European cultural heritage in a concentrated manner with a profound historical dimension. As each national library develops its own online systems to disseminate information about its collections, a myriad of information services across Europe is emerging. As there is no uniformity in the way users can acquire information about or gain access to these services, only a properly managed pan-European systematic guide can guarantee that all available services can be found and accessed adequately. Gabriel functions as such a guide by offering a single entry point to the libraries and their services, and by disseminating information about the national libraries in a uniform way.

Professional associations

One of the most effective professional associations for international co-operation is in the UK, where CILIP: the Chartered Institute of Library and Information Professionals, formerly The Library Association, has developed a system of bilateral agreements with a variety of countries, facilitating exchanges of staff and expertise as well as building links between particular libraries in the UK and other countries. Specific programmes have been developed in the past with the Baltic States, Hungary, Portugal and Romania, resulting in the establishment of bilateral links for staff training, management information and exchange of experiences and staff. In one case a Department of Library and Information Science has franchized its courses to an Eastern European country. The LA has also had a long-standing bilateral programme of co-operation with Germany and France, which has resulted in a number of informal links between libraries of different kinds.

The European Union

Without doubt, one of the most significant players in building regional co-operation in Europe has been the European Union, which for many years had a specific Telematics for Libraries Programme. The EU itself does not have a library programme as such in its political agenda, with the result that there is no objective other than to improve library services generally and also to facilitate co-operation between different libraries and between the library sector and other components of the industry. A very large amount of work was carried out by the European Commission in the libraries field under the Third and Fourth Framework Programmes for Research and Technological Development, Telematics for Libraries, from 1990 to 1998. While a considerable number of projects are still being supported under the Fourth Framework Programme, the EU is already working under the Fifth Framework Programme (1998–2002), where libraries are principally involved in the Multimedia Content and Tools area of the User-friendly Information Society IST Programme.

The Telematics for Libraries programme was co-ordinated by DG XIII/4 and supported 87 main projects and six platforms from 1990 onwards. Around 350 parties – about half of them libraries – were involved in the projects. It is worth noting that greater interaction has arisen between projects than would normally be expected. Both the profiles and the results of the projects varied widely, and they were reflected in many ways in Europe's libraries. Standards were developed (UNIMARC; EDIFACT), as were freeware tools, for example, in connection with the Z39.50 standard, and technical knowhow was transferred from area to area. One example was Project FACIT (Fast Automatic Conversion with Integrated Tools), which explored the use of OCR/ICR in retroconversion of catalogues with automatic error detection/correction and formating facilities. Information was gathered concerning the degree of maturity and usability of technical applications. Practical co-operation between libraries such as Computerised Bibliographic Record Actions (CoBRA) has been an important priority. Various platforms have played a vital role: European Copyright User Platform (ECUP) is of particular relevance as highly successful and resulting in a continuing programme of co-operation.

The value of the Telematics for Libraries programme was most apparent in the development of standards, the creation of prototypes and promotion of the use of technical solutions. It significantly increased co-operation among the libraries of European countries and indirectly also between library organizations. It has also increased co-operation between libraries and their commercial partners. All this has served to give libraries a higher profile, both at European level and in the Member States.

A major breakthrough in library co-operation in Europe was the introduction of a Draft European Directive on Copyright (European Commission, 1997). Opposition to some of the elements of this proposed legislation was so strong that a number of organizations banded together to form the European Fair Practice in Copyright Campaign (EFPICC). This brought together the European Consumers' Association, the European Association of Consumer Electronics Manufacturers, the European Bureau of Library, Information and Documentation Associations, the European Blind Union, the European Disability Forum and the International League of Societies for Persons with Mental Handicap – European Association. All campaigned vigorously against certain changes to European copyright law that would seriously hinder the interests of their members. It would be difficult to find a more diverse group of organizations working with libraries or, indeed, one that was nearly as effective. EFPICC eventually achieved many of the changes it wanted. The role of the European Bureau of Library, Information and Documentation Associations (EBLIDA) was crucial in this campaign as the European Union will not deal with national organizations in these circumstances and insists on a Europe-wide platform representing each sector. This required each national library association, as well as other representative bodies such as the Standing Conference of National and University Libraries (SCONUL) to work together to lobby the EU and its institutions. This has resulted in an ongoing debate about intellectual property, which is likely to be a continuing thread in library developments in the future. It has certainly served to establish EBLIDA as a regional force in library work to be reckoned with in the future. EBLIDA brings together many European, not just EU, members in a similar way to IFLA but its success in the copyright field may be its possible downfall. What can it find on which to focus that will continue the impetus? This is a major question for the future strategy of EBLIDA. The very fact that EBLIDA is seeking opinions on its future direction is significant and the organization is currently debating the way forward (EBLIDA, 2001).

Other regional organizations

Because of the unique nature of the European Union, which displays certain characteristics of a national government, international co-operation in Europe is more highly developed than anywhere else. A number of regional associations exist round the world, but their role is largely one of enabling members in a particular region to keep in touch. They certainly do offer opportunities, through workshops and conferences, for members to meet and identify possible areas of co-operation. Scarce funding, limited full-time staff capacity and volunteers scattered over large geographical areas all militate against expecting too much in these circumstances. In addition, it must be recognized that mere geographical proximity does not always mean that co-operation is possible or even desirable! Factors such as language or subject interests may be of more significance in library co-operation. Moreover, the varying political situation in any one area may make partnership difficult (Cornish, 1989). Mention should be made of the sterling work carried out by the Association of Caribbean University and Research Institution Libraries (ACURIL) in enabling libraries to learn about new IT developments and developing standard practices in this area. Other regional bodies working to promote co-operation include the Standing Conference of Eastern, Central and Southern African Librarians (SCESAL), the Congress of Southeast Asian Libraries (CONSAL) and the Pacific Islands Association of Libraries and Archives (PIALA).

The future of international co-operation

Libraries and their functions cannot be divorced from the 'real' world they serve and the changes taking place in the economic and political arena need to be considered when considering how the future might look.

First, many people claim that technological developments will ensure that international barriers come tumbling down. Information can be transferred so easily between countries that the concept of a 'national' library service will soon become meaningless. Therefore, international co-operation and partnership will continue to grow, with the inevitable consequence that more and more libraries will work together as well as working with partners outside the LIS area directly, such as software manufacturers, publishers and lawyers. Technology can, and will, facilitate much easier exchange of information, but will also enable the sharing of ideas, training and management skills.

Second, the globalization of trade should ensure that the library community in its widest sense benefits. Information as a commodity ought to be more easily traded and libraries should be in a position to share not only skills and expertise but also their actual collections. Mutual support initiatives can be more easily put in place and many possibilities explored that were impracticable because of sheer distance or the investment of time and travel necessary to achieve them.

There can be little doubt that many resource-sharing schemes will founder because of legal barriers such as copyright, Single Market legislation – which is prevalent in the EU but more likely to become global under the World Trade Organization (WTO) – and because of political opposition in some countries. WTO rules on national protection regulations may bring about a revolution in the way our libraries and other information services are operated and funded. Functions that are regarded at the moment as strictly the responsibility of local authorities, for example, public libraries and school libraries, or of universities, may become subject to international tender. Companies tendering for operations such as running the library may already have other commercial interests that have nothing to do with libraries. They may wish to develop co-operative schemes between the library and other parts of their commercial empire or with those geographical locations in which they already work, whether or not these are in the interests of the library service. Co-operation merely for the benefit of the library service could become a thing of the past.

Other pressures will also have to be taken into account. Earlier it was said that the international NGOs functioned largely because of the altruism of their members. In a world where budgets become progressively tighter, and questions about value for money are increasingly at the top of the agenda, how will libraries continue to justify expenditure (time, staff, consumables) in supporting such organizations? Where is the benefit to them or their employers?

The answer is surely in the topic discussed here. International co-operation just for its own sake cannot survive. But then, if it is for its own sake, perhaps it has no right to survive! Co-operation, whether local, national or international, should be of benefit to all those taking part, otherwise it is not co-operation at all but benevolence. This benefit should be of such significance or magnitude that anyone observing it will be struck by the value of what is being achieved in real terms. If we want international co-operation to continue we must practise it in such a way that it is its own advocate. Otherwise this chapter may become historical rather than actual in relevance.

References

AACR2 (1998) *Anglo-American cataloguing rules*, 2nd edn 1998 revision, London, Library Association Publishing.

Cornish, G. P. (1989) Interlending in the Caribbean: questions, problems and possible solutions, *Interlending and Document Supply*, **17** (2), 35–41.

EBLIDA (2001) *Strategy for the future*, EBLIDA, available at **www.eblida.org/strategy/main_strategy.htm**

European Commission (1997) *Proposal for a European Parliament and Council Directive on the harmonization of certain aspects of copyright and related rights in the information society*, COM (97) 628 final, Brussels, European Commission.

Gould, S. (1995) A voucher scheme to simplify payment for international interlibrary transactions, *Interlending and Document Supply*, **23** (1), 15–19.

International Council on Archives (2000) *ISAD(G) general international standard archival description*, 2nd edn, Paris, International Council on Archives.

Morales Campos, E. (1994) *Préstamo interbibliotecario entre Mexico y los Estados Unidos.* Paper presented at the 60th IFLA General Conference, Havana, Cuba, 1994, Paper 125-DOCDEL-2.

Acronyms

ACURIL	Association of Caribbean University, Research and Institutional Libraries
AHDS	Arts and Humanities Data Service
AIC	American Institute for Conservation
AIM25	Archives in London and the M25 area
ALA	American Library Association
ALL	Access to Libraries for Learning
ARL	Association of Research Libraries
ARLIS	Art Libraries Society
BL	British Library
BLCMP	Birmingham Libraries Co-operative Mechanisation Project
BLCPP	British Library Co-operation and Partnership Programme
BLDSC	British Library Document Supply Centre
BLLD	British Library Lending Division
BLRIC	British Library Research and Innovation Centre
BNB	British National Bibliography
BOPCRIS	British Official Publications Collaborative Reader Information Service
BRASTACS	Bradford Scientific, Technical and Commercial Services
BUCOP	British Union Catalogue of Periodicals
CAIRNS	Co-operative Academic Information Retrieval Network for Scotland
CALIM	Consortium of Academic Libraries in Manchester
CAMILEON	Creative Archiving at Michigan and Leeds: Emulating the Old and the New
CAVAL	Co-operative Action by Victorian Academic Libraries
CC–IW	Cydfenthyca Cymru – Interlending Wales
CCI	Canadian Conservation Institute
CDNL	Conference of Directors of National Libraries
Cedars	CURL Exemplars in Digital Archives

CENL	Conference of European National Librarians
CHEST	Combined Higher Education Software Team
CILIP	Chartered Institute of Library and Information Professionals (formerly The Library Association)
CLIR	Council on Library and Information Resources
CNI	Coalition for Networked Information
CoBRA	Computerised Bibliographic Record Actions
COC	Consortium of Consortia
CONARLS	Circle of Officers of National and Regional Library Systems
CONSAL	Congress of Southeast Asian Librarians
COPAC	CURL Online Public Access Catalogue
COPOL	Committee of Polytechnic Librarians
CRCDG	Centre de Recherches sur la Conservation des Documents Graphiques
CSERGE	Centre for Social and Economic Research on the Global Environment
CURL	Consortium of University Research Libraries
CWLIS	Consortium of Welsh Library and Information Services
DCMS	Department for Culture, Media and Sport
DG	Directorate General
DLF	Digital Library Federation
DNC	distributed national collection
DNER	Distributed National Electronic Resource
DNH	Department of National Heritage
DPC	Digital Preservation Coalition
EBLIDA	European Bureau of Library, Information and Documentation Associations
ECAI	Electronic Cultural Atlas Initiative
ECPA	European Commission on Preservation and Access
ECUP	European Copyright User Platform
EDIFACT	Electronic Data Interchange for Administration, Commerce and Transport
EEDA	East of England Development Agency
EFPICC	European Fair Practice in Copyright Campaign
EFTEC	Economics for the Environment Consultancy
e-Lib	Electronic Libraries Programme
ELISA	East of England Library and Information Services Development Agency

ESF	European Social Fund
EU	European Union
FACIT	Fast Automatic Conversion with Integrated Tools
FID	Fédération Internationale d'Information et de Documentation, *or* International Federation for Information and Documentation
GABRIEL	Gateway to Europe's National Libraries
GAELS	Glasgow Allied Electronically with Strathclyde: Information Environment for Engineering
HATII	Humanities Advanced Technology and Information Institute (University of Glasgow)
Hatrics	Hampshire technical, research industrial, commercial and scientific information
HEFCE	Higher Education Funding Council for England
HILT	High Level Thesaurus
HLF	Heritage Lottery Fund
IAML	International Association of Music Libraries, Archives and Documentation Centres
IATUL	International Association of Technological University Libraries
ICA	International Council on Archives
ICBS	International Committee of the Blue Shield
ICCROM	International Centre for the Study of the Preservation and the Restoration of Cultural Property, Rome
ICOLC	International Coalition of Library Consortia
ICOM	International Council on Museums
ICOMOS	International Council on Monuments and Sites
ICR	intelligent character recognition
ICT	information and communications technology
IDA	information development agency
IDP	International Dunhuang Project
IFLA	International Federation of Library Associations
IFLA-PAC	IFLA Core Programme for Preservation and Conservation
IIC	International Institute for Conservation of Historic and Artistic Works
IPC	Institute of Paper Conservation
ISBD	International Standard Bibliographic Description
isNTO	Information Services National Training Organisation
ISO	International Organization for Standardization
IST	information society technologies

IT	information technology
JANET	Joint Academic Network
JCEI	JISC Committee on Electronic Information
JISC	Joint Information Systems Committee
KB	Koninklijke Bibliotheek
LA	Library Association (now CILIP)
LACAP	Latin American Co-operative Acquisitions Plan
LAMDA	London and Manchester Document Access
LASER	London and South-East Library Region
LASh	Libraries Access Sunderland Scheme
LIBER	Ligue des Bibliothèques Européennes de Recherche
LIC	Library and Information Commission
LINC	Library and Information Co-operation Council
LIP	Library and Information Plan
LIS	library and information services
LISC (NI)	Library and Information Services Council (Northern Ireland)
LLDA	London Libraries Development Agency
MAGiC	Management of Access to Grey Literature Collections
MALIBU	Managing the Hybrid Library for the Benefit of Users
MAN	Metropolitan Area Network
MARC	Machine Readable Catalogue
MGC	Museums and Galleries Commission
MIMAS	Manchester InforMation & Associated Services
MRF	Master Reference File
NASA	National Aeronautics and Space Administration
NCL	National Central Library
NEDLIB	Networked European Deposit Library
NEMLAC	North East Museums, Libraries and Archives Council
NESLI	National Educational Site Licence Initiative
NFF	Non-formula Funding
NGO	non-governmental organization
NLLST	National Lending Library for Science and Technology
NOF	New Opportunities Fund
NPO	National Preservation Office
NWRLS	North Western Regional Library System
OAIS	Open Archival Information System
OCLC	Online Computer Library Center
OCR	optical character recognition

OPAC	Online Public Access Catalogue
OSTI	Office for Scientific and Technical Information
PADI	Preserving Access to Digital Information
PALS	Public and Academic Library Services
PAP	Preservation Administrators Panel (of the NPO)
PFI	Private Finance Initiative
PIALA	Pacific Islands Association of Libraries and Archives
PICA	Center for Library Automation
PLUS	Public Library User Surveys
PREMA	Prevention in Museums of Africa
PRESERV	RLG Preservation Program
PRO	Public Record Office
RASCAL	Research and Special Collections Available Locally
RCC	regional cultural consortium
RDA	regional development agency
RDN	Resource Discovery Network
REACH	Rationalised Economic Appraisal of Cultural Heritage
REDS	Regional Emergency Disaster Squad
RLG	Research Libraries Group
RLIN	Research Libraries Information Network
RLS	regional library system
RSLG	Research Support Libraries Group
RSLP	Research Support Libraries Programme
SAIL	Shropshire Access to Information for Learning
SAPIENS	Scottish Academic Periodicals: Implementing an Effective Networked Service
SCAD	Survey on Conservation of Asian Documents
SCECSAL	Standing Conference of Eastern, Central and Southern African Librarians
SCL	Society of Chief Librarians
SCN	Southern Conservation Network
SCOLD	Standing Committee on Legal Deposit
SCOLMA	Standing Conference on Library Materials on Africa
SCONE	Scottish Collections Network Extension
SCONUL	Society of College, National and University Libraries (previously Standing Conference of National and University Libraries)
ScoRe	Search Company Reports: a National Catalogue of Company Reports

SCRAN	Scottish Cultural Resources Area Network
SCURL	Scottish Confederation of University and Research Libraries
SELPIG	South East Libraries Performance Improvement Group
SEPIA	Safeguarding European Photographic Images for Access
SHAIR	Shropshire Access to Information Resources
SINTO	Sheffield Information Organisation
SLIC	Scottish Library and Information Council
SMSMA	Sharing Museums Skills Millennium Award Scheme
SPARC	Scholarly Publishing and Academic Resources Coalition
SPIS	Shared Preservation in Scotland
STEP	Science and Technology for Environmental Protection Initiative
STM	scientific, technical and medical
SUNCAT	Serials Union Catalogue
SWALCAP	South West Academic Libraries Co-operative Automation Project
SWRLS	South-West Regional Library System
TEL	The European Library
TLP–WM	The Libraries Partnership – West Midlandss
UAP	Universal Availability of Publications
UDC	Universal Decimal Classification
UDCC	Universal Decimal Classification Consortium
UGC	University Grants Committee
UKIRB	United Kingdom and Ireland Blue Shield Organisation
UKOLN	UK Office for Library and Information Networking
UNESCO	United Nations Educational, Scientific and Cultural Organization
UNIMARC	Universal Machine Readable Cataloguing
WARM	Widening Access to Resources in Merseyside
WLSP	World List of Scientific Periodicals
WM.CLAM	West Midlands Council for Libraries, Archives and Museums
WMRLS	West Midlands Regional Library System
WTO	World Trade Organization
YLSG	Yorkshire Libraries Strategy Group

Websites

Access to Archives
   www.a2a.pro.gov.uk/
ARLIS: the Art Libraries Society
   http://arlis.nal.vam.ac.uk/
Arts and Humanities Data Service
   http://ahds.ac.uk/
BIBLINK
   http://hosted.ukoln.ac.uk/biblink/
Bibliotheca universalis
   www.bl.uk/gabriel/bibliotheca-universalis/
British Library Co-operation and Partnership Programme
   www.bl.uk/concord/
British Official Publications Collaborative Reader Information Service
   www.bopcris.ac.uk/
Canadian Conservation Institute
   www.cci-icc.gc.ca/
Centre de Recherches sur la Conservation des Documents Graphiques
   www.crcdg.culture.fr/
Co-East
   www.co-east.net/
Combined Higher Education Software Team
   www.chest.ac.uk/
Conference of European National Librarians
   www.bl.uk/gabriel/en/cenl-general.html/
Conservation-NCCR
   www.jiscmail.ac.uk/lists/conservation-nccr.html
Conservation-Research
   www.jiscmail.ac.uk/lists/conservation-research.html
Consortium of Academic Libraries in Manchester
   www.calim.ac.uk/

Consortium of Welsh Library and Information Services
www.dils.aber.ac.uk/holi/cwlis/mission.htm
Co-operative Academic Information Retrieval Network for Scotland
http://cairns.lib.gla.ac.uk/
Co-operative Action by Victorian Academic Libraries
www.caval.edu.au/
Creative Archiving at Michigan and Leeds: Emulating the Old and the New
www.si.umich.edu/CAMILEON/
Culture Online
www.cultureonline.gov.uk/
CURL Exemplars for Digital Archives
www.curl.ac.uk/projects/cedars.html
CURL Taskforce on Resource Management
www.curl.ac.uk/about/GroupsRM.html
Cydfenthyca Cymru — Interlending Wales
http://seren.newi.ac.uk/cciw/main.htm
Digital Imaging Tutorial
www.library.cornell.edu/preservation/tutorial/contents.html
Digital-Preservation
www.jiscmail.ac.uk/lists/digital-preservation.html
Digital Preservation Coalition
www.jisc.ac.uk/dner/preservation/prescoalition.html
Early Buddhist Manuscripts Project
http://depts.washington.edu/ebmp/
East of England Library and Information Services Development Agency
www.elisa.org.uk/
Electronic Beowulf
www.bl.uk/diglib/beowulf/
Electronic Cultural Atlas Initiative
www.ecai.org/
Electronic Libraries Programme
www.ukoln.ac.uk/services/elib/
European Commission on Preservation and Access
www.knaw.nl/ecpa/
European Consortium of Innovative Universities
www.eciu.org/
Fathom
www.fathom.com/

Glasgow Allied Electronically with Strathclyde: Information Environment for Engineering
http://gaels.lib.gla.ac.uk/
Glasgow Digital Library
http://gdl.cdlr.strath.ac.uk/
Hatrics: the Southern Information Network
www.hatrics.org.uk/
High Level Thesaurus
http://hilt.cdlr.strath.ac.uk/
Humanities Advanced Technology and Information Institute (University of Glasgow)
www.hatii.arts.gla.ac.uk/index.htm
IFLA Core Programme for Preservation and Conservation
www.ifla.org/VI/4/pac.htm
Institute of Paper Conservation
www.ipc.org.uk/
International Centre for the Study of the Preservation and the Restoration of Cultural Property, Rome
www.iccrom.org/eng/
International Conference on Monuments and Sites
www.icomos.org/
International Council on Archives
www.ica.org/
International Council on Museums
www.icom.org
International Dunhuang Project
http://idp.bl.uk/
International Institute for Conservation of Historic and Artistic Works
www.iiconservation.org/
JISCmail
www.jiscmail.ac.uk/
Koninklijke Bibliotheek (digital archiving)
www.kb.nl/kb/resources/frameset_kenniscentrum-en.html
LASh: Libraries Access Sunderland Scheme
www.nyrlas.nhs.uk/NHSlibrariansyork/sld013.htm
Library and Information Services Council (Northern Ireland)
www.liscni.co.uk/

Ligue des Bibliothèques Européennes de Recherche (Preservation Division)
www.kb.dk/guests/intl/liber/division/preserv/
London Libraries Development Agency
www.llda.org.uk/
M25 Consortium
www.m25lib.ac.uk/
M25 Consortium: Disaster Control Planning Site
www.m25lib.ac.uk/M25dcp/
MALIBU
www.kcl.ac.uk/humanities/cch/malibu/
Management of Access to Grey Literature Collections
www.magic.ac.uk/
Manchester InforMation & Associated Services
www.mimas.ac.uk/
Metamorfoze
www.kb.nl/coop/metamorfoze/
National Museum Directors' Conference
www.nationalmuseums.org.uk/
National Preservation Office
www.bl.uk/services/preservation/national.html
Networked European Deposit Library
www.kb.nl/coop/nedlib/
New Opportunities Fund
www.nof.org.uk/
NEWSPLAN
www.bl.uk/collections/nplan.html
NEWSPLAN 2000 project
www.newsplan2000.org/
NOF-digitisation
www.nof-digitise.org/
North East Museums, Libraries and Archives Council
www.nemlac.co.uk/
North Western Regional Library System
www.nwrls.org.uk/
People's Network
www.peoplesnetwork.gov.uk/
Preserving Access to Digital Information
www.nla.gov.au/padi/

Prevention in Museums in Sub-Saharan Africa
  www.iccrom.org/eng/activ/p10pmae.htm
Public Library of Science
  www.publiclibraryofscience.org/
Public Library User Surveys (PLUS)
  www.ipf.co.uk/plus/default.htm
Rationalised Economic Appraisal of Cultural Heritage
  http://projects.bre.co.uk/REACH/
Research Libraries Group Preservation Program
  http://lyra.rlg.org/preserv/
Research Support Libraries Programme
  www.rslp.ac.uk/
Resource: the Council for Museums Archives and Libraries
  www.resource.gov.uk/
Revelation
  www.is.bham.ac.uk/rslp/revelation.htm
RIDING: Gateway to Yorkshire libraries
  www.riding.ac.uk/
Safeguarding European Photographic Images for Access
  www.knaw.nl/ecpa/sepia/
SAIL: Shropshire Access to Information for Learning
  www.s-cat.ac.uk/sail/
Scholarly Publishing and Academic Resources Coalition
  www.arl.org/sparc/
Scottish Academic Periodicals: Implementing an Effective Networked Service
  http://cdlr.strath.ac.uk/projects/projects-sapiens.html
Scottish Cultural Resources Area Network
  www.scran.ac.uk/
Scottish Library and Information Council
  www.slainte.org.uk/Slic/slichome.htm
Search Company Reports: a National Catalogue of Company Reports
  www.score.ac.uk/
Shared Preservation in Scotland
  http://scurl.ac.uk/projects/spis/
SINTO: The Sheffield Information Organisation
  www.shu.ac.uk/sinto/
Southern Conservation Network
  www.soton.ac.uk/~conserve/index.htm

Survey on Conservation of Asian Documents
www.bodley.ox.ac.uk/scad/
The European Library
www.europeanlibrary.org/
The Libraries Partnership — West Midlands
www.tlp-wm.org.uk/
Touchstone
www.bham.ac.uk/touchstone/
UK Office for Library and Information Networking
http://ukoln.bath.ac.uk/
United Kingdom and Ireland Blueshield Organisation
www.bl.uk/services/preservation/blueshield/
Universitas 21
www.universitas.edu.au/
West Midlands Council for Libraries, Archives and Museums
www.wm-museums.co.uk/culture/wmclam.html
Yorkshire Libraries Strategy Group
www.ylsg.org.uk/

Index